DIFFERENTIATED

LITERACY
COACHING

ASCD MEMBER BOOK

Many ASCD members received this book as a
member benefit upon its initial release.

Learn more at: **www.ascd.org/memberbooks**

DIFFERENTIATED

LITERACY
COACHING

Scaffolding for Student and Teacher Success

MARY CATHERINE MORAN

Association for Supervision and Curriculum Development
Alexandria, Virginia USA

Association for Supervision and Curriculum Development
1703 N. Beauregard St. • Alexandria, VA 22311-1714 USA
Phone: 800-933-2723 or 703-578-9600 • Fax: 703-575-5400
Web site: www.ascd.org • E-mail: member@ascd.org
Author guidelines: www.ascd.org/write

Gene R. Carter, *Executive Director;* Nancy Modrak, *Publisher;* Julie Houtz, *Director of Book Editing & Production;* Katie Martin, *Project Manager;* Greer Beeken, *Graphic Designer;* Valerie Younkin, *Desktop Publishing Specialist;* Dina Murray Seamon, *Production Specialist/Team Lead*

All Web links in this book are correct as of the publication date below but may have become inactive or otherwise modified since that time. If you notice a deactivated or changed link, please e-mail books@ascd.org with the words "Link Update" in the subject line. In your message, please specify the Web link, the book title, and the page number on which the link appears.

ASCD Member Book, No. FY08-3 (December 2007, P). ASCD Member Books mail to Premium (P) and Comprehensive (C) members on this schedule: Jan., PC; Feb., P; Apr., PC; May, P; July, PC; Aug., P; Sept., PC; Nov., PC; Dec., P.

PAPERBACK ISBN: 978-1-4166-0623-9   ASCD product #107053
Also available as an e-book through ebrary, netLibrary, and many online booksellers (see Books in Print for the ISBNs).

Quantity discounts for the paperback edition only: 10–49 copies, 10%; 50+ copies, 15%; for 1,000 or more copies, call 800-933-2723, ext. 5634, or 703-575-5634. For desk copies: member@ascd.org.

Library of Congress Cataloging-in-Publication Data
Moran, Mary Catherine, 1954-

  Differentiated literacy coaching : scaffolding for student and teacher success / Mary Catherine Moran.
    p. cm.
  Includes bibliographical references and index.
  ISBN 978-1-4166-0623-9 (pbk. : alk. paper) 1. Reading teachers--In-service training. 2. Mentoring in education. 3. Teaching teams. 4. Reading. 5. Lesson planning. I. Title.

  LB2844.1.R4M67 2007
  371.14'8--dc22

                                                                                  2007033134

18 17 16 15 14 13 12 11 10 09 08 07   1 2 3 4 5 6 7 8 9 10 11 12

For my loving parents,
Polly and Charlie Moran

You passed on to me a love of learning,
a sense of community spirit, and an intellectual
curiosity about the world around me. For this
and for so many gifts I cannot begin to measure,
I thank you from the bottom of my heart.

Differentiated Literacy Coaching
Scaffolding for Student and Teacher Success

Appendixes

Preface

My first experience with coaching was in 1977. I was a novice educator in Northern Vermont, newly hired to teach special education in a K–8 building. Although 30 years have passed, I can clearly remember the excitement I felt in the weeks leading up to the first day of school. I spent hours planning, reviewing my students' files, poring over books, and preparing "perfect" lessons. I imagined the seamless and happy collaboration that would take place between me and my students' classroom teachers. When the first day of school arrived, I was ready.

As you might guess, it didn't take more than a few hours for reality to set in. My perfect lessons, which I'd developed without knowing the living and breathing students I'd be teaching, weren't quite so perfect after all. I was responsible for educating individuals who didn't quite match my preconceived notions. What's more, the easy collaboration with colleagues that I'd envisioned was complicated by me not knowing a soul on the faculty, and by the fact that my classroom was a trailer located at the far end of the blacktop playground. Panic replaced enthusiasm.

Thank heavens for the resiliency of youth and for the Vermont State Department of Education. As a new special education teacher, I was assigned a coach who provided "job-embedded" professional development. Sara was not much older than I, but she had the benefit of a master's degree and five years of teaching experience. She visited my classroom to help me review student data, plan instruction, and reflect on lessons learned. Those early days of support and focused, professional learning made all the difference for me, the classroom teachers I worked with, and my students. It also greatly influenced my perspective on the value of coaching. Later in my career, I came to be a mentor and coach to others.

I began to develop the Literacy Coaching Continuum Model described in this book in 1999, in collaboration with my colleague Elizabeth (Tiz) Powers, senior project associate from the former Region III Comprehensive Center at George Washington University, now known as the Mid-Atlantic Comprehensive Center. Over the past seven years, we have worked with many literacy coaches who have generously shared with us what their jobs involve, what challenges they face, and what professional supports they have found to be the most helpful in meeting the needs of a variety of individual teachers, each of whom is responsible for ensuring the literacy learning of living, breathing, individual students. Tiz and I have reflected on and refined our professional learning framework, which provides the guidelines and support a literacy coach needs to meet the challenges of the position.

I would like to take this opportunity to thank Tiz, whose insight and generosity have made this book a richer document. I look forward to many more years of happy and productive collaboration. I would also like to thank Scott Willis, director of Books Acquisition and Development at ASCD. He was my first official introduction to the world of publishing, and I could not have asked for a more respectful and enthusiastic mentor. Thanks also to my editor, Katie Martin, who kept me focused, on time, and thoroughly engaged in the editing process. Finally, Darcy Bradley first showed an interest in this book as a worthwhile project. Her encouraging e-mails were instrumental in shaping the early stages of the book.

Various forms in this book are available for download in a password-protected PDF format from the ASCD Web site: www.ascd.org. Follow the Publications link to the Books page, click on "Browse by Title," and then select this book's title. To access the PDFs, enter the password *ASCD107053* when prompted. I hope you will use these forms and all the information you find in this book. Share them with your colleagues, look up the primary resources I cite, and dig deeper for a clearer understanding of what you want your literacy coaching program to achieve. There is no "perfect" program or comprehensive cookbook for success, but there are some reliable recipes and guidelines for assembling them into appropriate menus. With some personalized tweaking, you can deliver a program that will satisfy the diverse professional learning needs of your colleagues and the literacy learning needs of their students.

PART I

FOUNDATIONS

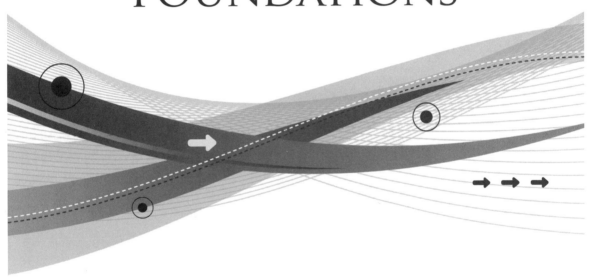

1

The Context for a Literacy
Coaching Continuum

With the ever-increasing focus on reading achievement in schools today, many districts are hiring literacy coaches to provide embedded professional learning opportunities for their teachers. Coaching holds great promise as a tool to increase teachers' content knowledge. It's an essential ingredient in educators' efforts to increase student achievement, and it has the potential to nurture a culture of academic focus by valuing current professional knowledge and extending and enhancing effective pedagogical practice.

The use of literacy coaches is not without controversy, however, and there are a number of reasons for this, including uncertainty about the purpose of literacy coaching, multiple interpretations of the title and role of a literacy coach, and the varying qualifications of the individuals hired to provide the coaching support.

Some educators perceive coaching as punitive—a remedial service for those who aren't teaching up to standard. Others view the coaching experience as evaluation under the guise of support or as directives in reflective disguise (the wolf in grandma's clothing). Still others consider coaching an unnecessary distraction from the daily business of teaching and suggest that coaches reserve their time for "teachers who really need it."

Clearly, one job of a literacy coach is to help school staff grapple with the role itself. *What is a literacy coach, and what exactly does one do?* Without a defined role, coaches may hear comments along these lines: "I've been teaching for a long time. Why don't you spend time with the people who really need your help?" At a recent meeting I attended, one teacher even referred to coaching as an "expensive waste of time."

Further testament to the general confusion about the role of the literacy coach is the variety of names the position goes by. In a recent review of the literature, I came across the following monikers: *reading coach, expert coach, technical coach, cognitive coach, peer coach, collegial coach, content-focused coach, collaborative coach, design coach, instructional coach, academic coach,* and *reflective coach.* Perhaps the International Reading Association's *Standards for Reading Professionals* (2007) can provide some clarity? This document defines a reading or literacy coach as

> a reading specialist who focuses on providing professional development for teachers by providing them with the additional support needed to implement various instructional programs and practices. They provide essential leadership for the school's entire literacy program by helping create and supervise a long-term staff development process that supports both the development and implementation of the literacy program over months and years. These individuals need to have experiences that enable them to provide effective professional development for the teachers in their schools. (Category III, bullet 2)

I like this definition. It acknowledges the necessary qualifications of the literacy coach, addresses the ongoing nature of the position, and recognizes that an effective coach must be proactive and have experience working with adult learners.

I won't presume to endorse a particular term for what coaches should be called, but I believe strongly that the *purpose* of a literacy coaching program and the *roles* of the coaches within that program must be thoughtfully considered and articulated before implementation. When a school considers adding the position of literacy coach to the roster, the first questions that should be discussed are "Why hire a literacy coach?" and "What is the goal of the position?" Often the coach is already on board, and the questions have yet to be asked, much less answered.

When considering and constructing your own response to these key questions, you may find it helpful to review other coaching program policies. Consider the Collaborative Coaching and Learning (CCL) model, launched by the Boston Public Schools in 1996 under the leadership of Superintendent Thomas Payzant. In launching the model, the district's purpose was to reduce professional isolation and ensure the integration of research-based practice in classrooms. The CCL framework features a six-week cycle of inquiry focused on instructional strategies. Inquiry teams are composed of a content coach, teachers, and the principal. Additional support includes a weekly lab practicum during which the coach, teachers, and principal take turns teaching and afterward discuss their observations (pre-conference, demonstrations, debrief). Content coaches also visit individual classrooms to support the implementation of the instructional strategies. The four main components of the CCL model—classroom experience, reflection and inquiry, feedback, and theory—exemplify what Linda Darling-Hammond and Milbrey W. McLaughlin (1995) highlight as an essential feature of effective professional development: "It must engage teachers in the concrete tasks of teaching, assessment, observation, and reflection that illuminate the process of learning and development" (p. 598).

Another model worth noting is the Arkansas Comprehensive Literacy Model, (ACLM), a partnership between the University of Arkansas at Little Rock, the Arkansas Department of Education, and Arkansas elementary schools. It features a schoolwide design for ensuring that all children achieve literacy proficiency by the end of 3rd grade. A planned extension of the ACLM to middle and high schools is in the pilot stage. Within the ACLM model, literacy coaching is 1 of 10 components identified as essential to the process, along with a curriculum for literacy, model classrooms, high standards, accountability, early intervention, professional development, a well-designed literacy plan, technology that includes networking opportunities, and the spotlighting of schools that are achieving high results. Coaches make sure that components of a K–3 reading program—including phonemic awareness, phonics, fluency, vocabulary, comprehension, and the writing process—are implemented with fidelity.

Successful literacy programs such as Boston's Collaborative Coaching and Learning model and Arkansas's Comprehensive Literacy Model underscore the importance of having an identified purpose and clearly defined roles and responsibilities. After all, if the literacy coach or administrator is confused about the roles and responsibilities of the position, why should we be surprised when teachers fail to embrace the model with enthusiasm? If our coaching model is designated as an intervention for some rather than an opportunity for all, why should we be surprised when teachers see the program as corrective in nature?

A report exploring the various roles and responsibilities of literacy coaches (Deussen, Coskie, Robinson, & Autio, 2007) may be a helpful document to consult as you wrestle with these determinations yourself. The authors analyzed Reading First data from five western states to determine how coaches allocated time, performed tasks, and described their responsibilities. As a result of their research, the authors classify coaches into five distinct groupings: "data-oriented, student-oriented, managerial, and two teacher-oriented categories, one that works largely with individual teachers and another that works with groups" (p. 4). Reviewing and reflecting on the distinctions between these definitions will be a helpful step in determining what you most value in terms of the role of literacy coaches in your model of professional learning.

Three Essential Principles of Coaching

The primary goal of literacy coaching is to improve student learning. Meeting this goal requires an understanding of, and attention to, research on effective district, school, and teacher practices, including a *guaranteed and viable curriculum* and *challenging goals and effective feedback* (Marzano, 2003).

Within the overarching goal of improved student achievement are three essential principles of coaching:

1. Coaching should help establish a school culture that recognizes collaboration as an asset.

2. Coaching should develop individual and group capacity to engage in creative problem solving and self-reflection.

3. Coaching should provide a continuum of professional learning opportunities to support adults in their acquisition and use of specific knowledge, skills, and strategies.

Let's examine each of these principles more closely.

Recognizing Collaboration as an Asset

Teaching is an intellectually challenging vocation much too important and complex to do in isolation. In teaching, two (or more) heads *are* better than one. Part of this process of acculturation involves embracing the notion that learning is a social activity (Vygotsky, 1978) that requires community engagement for renewal.

A few years ago, a teacher friend of mine decided to pursue a new career in counseling. Within a few years, she had completed a master's degree in counseling and begun part-time work at a local hospital. When I talked with her about the differences between professional learning in education and professional learning in the medical field, she described an ongoing process of staff support at her clinic called "case review." In essence, this process involved each counselor taking turns to share a case study and then having guided conversations with peers about the information presented. The same process would be very helpful in her school setting, she said, because it would provide an opportunity for the clinician (teacher) to thoughtfully consider a client (student), to review the care (instruction) provided to date, and to summarize the data she had collected to present to her colleagues for the consideration of next steps.

Some readers will recognize this process of shared practice; examples of the process do exist in some school settings. I suggest, however, that the recurring and shared use of case studies is a limited practice in education, even though we know that teachers benefit from this form of reflective collaboration (Feagin, Orum, & Sjoberg, 1991; Hammerness, Shulman, & Darling-Hammond, 2000; Shulman, 1991). Hiebert, Gallimore, and Stigler (2002) note that

> Teachers and educators around the country are beginning to see that the goal of improving teaching—improving students' opportunities to learn—can only be reached by a path that the United States has never taken before. This new path moves educators away from a view of teaching as a solitary activity, owned personally by each teacher. It moves them towards a view of teaching as a professional activity open to collective observations, study, and improvement. It invites ordinary teachers to recognize and accept the responsibility for improving not only their own practice, but the shared practice of the profession. For this new path to be traveled, however, teachers will need to open their classroom doors, and rather than evaluating each other, begin studying their practices as a professional responsibility common to all. (p. 1)

Developing Capacity for Creative Problem Solving and Self-Reflection

By developing individual and group capacity to engage in creative problem solving and self-reflection, faculty members are better able to approach teaching as a series of challenges we *respond* to, rather than a series of challenges we *react* to. This renewable form of collaborative energy also provides for authentic and ongoing evaluation to inform and refine subsequent practice in our teaching and our professional learning.

As any new educator (or seasoned educator in a new situation) knows, *reacting* is all too common. For me, the term *react* conjures up memories of classroom occurrences that would just happen out of the blue, without any foresight on my part. Some days it seemed that all I could do was deal with situations as they happened, take a deep breath, and do the very same thing the next day. Everything was new. As a consequence, I didn't have the resiliency to forecast and prepare for any eventualities, let alone all of them.

Of course, not even those of us who have years of experience and professional learning under our belts can be prepared for *everything*. I can say, though, that after nearly 30 years of teaching and learning, my adaptive reflexes are more instinctive; judicious response has largely replaced reaction. This doesn't mean that I don't still have wholly reactive moments. However, I recover from them much more quickly than I once did.

Providing a Continuum of Learning Opportunities

Gone are the days of menu shopping for workshop flavors of the month: "Please check the box next to the topic that holds the most interest for YOU." We now understand more clearly that our needs as teachers are met when we have the professional capacity to meet the needs of our students. We know that we can make better decisions if we have a comprehensive understanding of research and undertake a collaborative review of the data. As Mike Schmoker (1999) noted, "Data are to goals what signposts are to travelers; data are not end points, but are essential to reaching them—the signposts on the road to school improvement" (p. 36).

When determining what data we need to consider in our collaborative review and analysis, it helps to have a conceptual framework to guide us. I use one developed by the Southern California Comprehensive Center's Reading Success Network, which categorizes data into three types: outcome, demographic, and process.

Outcome data describe how a student or a group of students is doing at a particular point in time. They provide a way to communicate the acquisition of skills, knowledge, and attitudes. Examples of outcome data include tests (e.g., teacher-developed, state, and national), teacher observations, classroom work, portfolios, and interviews. *Demographic data* provide information that can improve our understanding of our students and their unique needs. Examples of demographic data include gender, language proficiency, attendance records, mobility rates, and family configuration. *Process data* emerge from efforts to promote student achievement and include variables that educators have some control over, such as interventions, textbooks, professional development initiatives, assessment practices, teacher experience, special programs, and our expectations for students.

A critical aspect of any comprehensive discussion of data is how we plan to apply research-based knowledge about best practice when working with our own students.

Determining Program Focus

With the three essential principles of coaching in mind, I want to turn to the question of an individual coaching program's objectives: What are the skills and proficiencies that the coaching aims to help teachers acquire? What is the specific instructional and curricular content they will be asked to implement in an effort to improve their students' achievement?

Deciding on a focus requires a great deal of finesse. How individuals interpret data is influenced by personal perspective and experience. While I might interpret errors in oral reading as a child's over-reliance on context clues, another teacher might ascribe it to the child's difficulty recognizing specific letter combinations. False beliefs or hunches about specific students or groups of students are more likely to be challenged through the collective lens of collaborative discussion. This is important because our decisions about appropriate instruction and interventions are guided by our discussions about root cause.

In a four-year case study focusing on data use in five low-performing urban high schools, Lachat and Smith (2005) found that collaborative inquiry on data use organized around a series of guided questions "is a potent strategy for building staff skills and keeping the focus on student learning and achievement" (p. 343). They also found that literacy coaches were instrumental in providing follow-up assistance to various data users in the schools, and in motivating teachers to use data to inform instructional decisions.

The value of collaboration in data discussions does not diminish with experience. Even as a veteran educator, I rely on the insights and experiences of my colleagues to negotiate my review of outcomes. I consider any contradiction of my interpretations an asset that will help me to round out my picture of what happened (both positive and negative), why it happened, and what I can do about it the next time around. For this reason, the collection and *collaborative* analysis of data should be an ongoing component of a coaching program. As noted in *The Secretary's Fourth Annual Report on Teacher Quality* (Westat, 2005), "teachers need the skills to organize, describe, and interpret data" (p. 11). Coaches are in a position to facilitate the ongoing collection and subsequent discussion of the pieces of the data puzzle so that decisions about program focus can be made in full awareness of what students can and can't do and which instructional approaches and curricular emphases, according to the research on literacy and learning, are most likely to be effective. Revisiting instructional decisions and coaching objectives on a regular basis helps program participants monitor, refine, and modify practices in light of any new information. This accretion of knowledge supports better instructional planning for students.

Please note that to expedite and ensure the regular collection and analysis of data, it's a good idea to establish consistency of practice throughout the coaching program. The data collection and analysis process should include assessing the effectiveness of the professional learning activities and the instructional interventions applied in the classroom in terms of their subsequent impact on student achievement.

In *Student Achievement Through Staff Development,* Bruce Joyce and Beverly Showers (2002) point out that there's no guarantee that professional development initiatives, even ones based on solid data and research, will translate into improved student learning. Simply replacing good practice with a good innovation is unlikely to result in an *increase* in student learning. If it is gain we seek, the innovation has to "up the ante" by

- Elevating what is taught, how it is taught, and the social climate of the school;
- Significantly affecting what is taught, how it is taught, and the social climate in the clinical sense that student behavior really changes to a considerable degree; and
- Providing opportunities for student learning to be studied continuously and diagnostically. (pp. 5–6)

Elsewhere in their book, Joyce and Showers provide concrete examples of how to measure the effectiveness of professional learning and optimize potential for growth in student achievement.

Generally speaking, when it comes to establishing a coaching program's focus, there is a tendency to try to take on too much at one time. Always remember that the goal of coaching is not to help teachers develop discrete skills that are relevant in only a limited number of scenarios but to advance knowledge and applications that teachers can and will generalize to other settings and situations. If our aim is to improve student learning by supporting collaboration among teachers and enhancing their creative problem solving through reflection, we can do this just as well (or better, actually) by targeting a strategic number of objectives explicitly relevant to those teachers. For example, if reading fluency is a focus, it would be important for teachers to learn the procedure for implementing and assessing repeated readings (a tool for building student fluency). The primary objective, however, is to engage teachers in reflective discussions about the method and its impact on student achievement:

- Do the students understand the purpose of the fluency training and how the process will improve their reading?
- Did the teacher effectively pre-teach the routine to the students?

• Were the reading passages the teacher selected effective, or should alternative materials be considered?

• Did this explicit instruction result in an increase in comprehension?

It's not feasible for a literacy coach to focus on teaching every teacher the discrete skills necessary to use every instructional tool available; a better plan is to facilitate teachers' deliberate and careful consideration of what they do and why they do it. Over time, this integration of reflection will generalize to other instructional routines, tools, and content that teachers may choose to incorporate into their classroom. Joyce and Showers (2002) agree. They suggest that "a faculty is much better positioned to change something if it can focus on a top priority in a way that simultaneously acknowledges both the presence and importance of everything on the list and the near impossibility of addressing all of them effectively at one time" (p. 5).

Catherine Snow, Peg Griffin, and M. Susan Burns (2005) offer professional learning recommendations specific to the development of literacy educators in their book *Knowledge to Support the Teaching of Reading: Preparing Teachers for a Changing World.* These authors discuss growth in expertise in the context of a teacher's career, from novice to seasoned professional. They consider the knowledge base and effective implementation of literacy practices in the context of changes that occur over time through the lens of adult learning theory. They articulate levels of *increasing progressive differentiation* of knowledge, correlated with points in a teacher's career evolution. Joyce and Showers (2002) articulate a similar understanding of the developmental and progressive nature of skill development in their "levels of transfer" (p. 102). See Figure 1.1 for a comparison of these two developmental continuums.

The usable knowledge that teachers need at various junctures and the considerations of what scaffolds of support should be provided to maximize learning at each level have far-reaching implications for the literacy coach and teachers. The information in Figure 1.1 provides a good start for collaborative discussion.

Determining Program Scope

A second key consideration is the scope of the literacy coaching program: Who will receive coaching? The entire staff? Certain teachers only? Program funding and resources usually factor in this decision about scope.

To make the most of limited coaching resources, some schools identify specific grade levels for coaching support, an approach that naturally limits the number of teachers that a coach is assigned to work with. Other schools opt to target particular

Figure 1.1 Comparison of Two Developmental Continuums	
Levels of Transfer **(Joyce & Showers, 2002)**	**Increasing Progressive Differentiation** **and Career Points** **(Snow et al., 2005)**
Imitative Use The teacher performs an exact replication of lessons demonstrated in training settings.	*Declarative Knowledge* (Preservice Teacher) The teacher can answer questions on a test about what to do in a classroom under certain circumstances.
Mechanical Use The teacher may use the same practice in another activity, but types of implementation show little variation.	*Situated, Can-Do Procedural Knowledge* (Apprentice Teacher) The teacher knows what to do in a classroom under certain (and predictable) circumstances and with support from a master teacher.
Routine Use The teacher can identify specific models of teaching with certain activities, types of lessons, and objectives.	*Stable, Procedural Knowledge* (Novice Teacher) The teacher can plan, implement, and monitor the instruction under "normal circumstances."
Integrated Use The teacher understands how a concept or strategy can be used in other areas of application.	*Expert, Adaptive Knowledge* (Experienced Teacher) The teacher can respond to a full array of instructional challenges under a variety of circumstances.
Executive Use The teacher shows a complete understanding and comfort level with the theories underlying various models of learning. As a consequence, the teacher is able to select specific models and combinations of models for objectives within a unit and across subject areas.	*Reflective, Organized, Analyzed Knowledge* (Master Teacher) The teacher has enough experience to analyze, evaluate, and make choices about instruction and assessment under varying circumstances with a wide range of students.

teachers for coaching. Too often, determining who will and who will not receive coaching relies on a deficit-style model built on identifying which teachers have problems that must be remediated in order for children to learn. It's true that this kind of targeted approach may help to address an administrative challenge by reducing the number of teachers that a coach must work with. However, if staff members come to see the coaching program as an intervention for some rather than an opportunity for all, there can be negative reverberations for the entire school community. This sets up a scenario in which teachers are reluctant to ask for support and guidance and begin to view professional learning opportunities as punitive.

A better solution is to limit the focus of the coaching program to a strategic set of objectives *and* to provide a continuum of customized professional learning opportunities to meet the varied needs of teachers. Via the continuum, the coach can play a direct role in the learning opportunities or facilitate these through shared leadership.

A continuum of coaching makes it possible to provide precisely what professionals need to evolve in their practice—a "just right" combination of challenging and respectful learning opportunities that the teachers themselves had a hand in creating. This option represents a more sensible allocation of coaching time and energy, avoiding the one-size-fits-all mentality that shapes so much professional development.

The Literacy Coaching Continuum

The Literacy Coaching Continuum (see Figure 1.2) is a structure for the kind of participatory professional learning that integrates fundamentals of adult education theory, provides scaffolds according to the needs of individual teachers, and respects and builds on the knowledge that teachers bring to the table. It is a conceptual framework for organizing, managing, assessing, and sharing information about literacy coaching efforts.

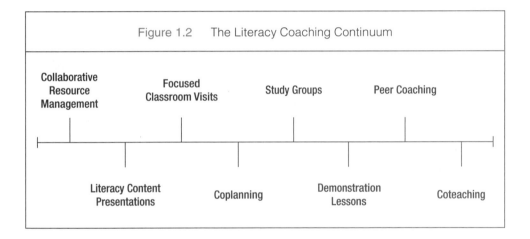

Figure 1.2   The Literacy Coaching Continuum

As shown in Figure 1.3, the continuum presents eight differentiated learning formats for coaching: (1) collaborative resource management, (2) literacy content presentations, (3) focused classroom visits, (4) coplanning, (5) study groups, (6) demonstration lessons, (7) peer coaching, and (8) coteaching. It assumes that there is a *progression* in the intensity of learning supports that are necessary to sustain a teacher's efforts to become a more reflective practitioner. For example, the scaffolding provided in resource management (at one end of the continuum) is far less intrusive than the assistance that would be apparent in coteaching (at the other end of the continuum).

Figure 1.3	A Closer Look at the Literacy Coaching Continuum	
Learning Format	**Description**	**Potential Roles of the Literacy Coach**
Collaborative Resource Management	The literacy coach works with teachers to become familiar with and tap into available resources. This is an opportunity for rich conversation about instruction, grouping, and differentiated instruction.	Resource person, collaborator, encourager
Literacy Content Presentations	The literacy coach provides content knowledge and fosters collaboration. This format ensures that all teachers are on the same page in terms of information, procedures, best practice, and other matters.	Facilitator, expert, resource person
Focused Classroom Visits	The literacy coach provides teachers the opportunity to observe a particular teaching method, learn how other teachers organize for instruction, and develop an understanding of what is expected at other grade levels.	Facilitator, resource person
Coplanning	Teachers work together to review current data and plan instruction. This might include discussion on grouping options, assessment results, and specific lesson planning.	Resource person, collaborator, encourager
Study Groups	A group of educators meets on a regular basis to discuss issues relevant to their teaching. The range of study group options includes job-alike, book study, and action research.	Facilitator, mediator, resource person
Demonstration Lessons	The literacy coach demonstrates particular teaching methods to teachers who are less familiar with these methods or less confident about using them.	Expert, consultant, presenter
Peer Coaching	This is the traditional coaching model whereby the literacy coach observes the classroom teacher and provides feedback during a debriefing session.	Expert, encourager, voice
Coteaching	The classroom teacher and the literacy coach plan a lesson together and share responsibility for the lesson's implementation and follow-up.	Collaborator, encourager, voice

Source: Developed by M. C. Moran and Elizabeth Powers.

Let me put the word *intrusive* in context. I use this term to indicate the extent of the coach's involvement in the actual teaching routine and the potential impact of that involvement on a teacher's sense of comfort. A coach who is working with a teacher on resource management will have less direct involvement in the teaching of a lesson than will one who is coteaching a lesson. Therefore, resource management is less intrusive than coteaching. The Literacy Coaching Continuum's differentiated formats of professional learning acknowledge that teachers are individuals who need and want various kinds of support depending upon content, circumstances, personal experience, and timing.

Gersten, Morvant, and Brengelman (1995) use a telling description of this notion in the title of an article published in *Exceptional Children*: "Close to the Classroom Is Close to the Bone: Coaching as a Means to Translate Research into Classroom Practice." These authors studied coaching as a way to translate research into classroom practice and found that teachers felt anxiety when change efforts involved an observation and coaching process. This reaction was especially evident with inexperienced teachers, although even veteran educators reported being nervous when another adult spent time in their classroom. The closer coaching gets to day-to-day classroom reality, the more likely it will be "close to the bone"—near those sensitive areas of practice that affect a teacher's sense of self-esteem and professional standing.

Choosing the Right Tools

The design of the Literacy Coaching Continuum is not intended to suggest that the scaffolds or formats are strictly linear (moving from one to the next without recursive intent). It does imply gradients in terms of support provided and the level of self-reflection required in each format.

The visual representation of the continuum is intended to encourage conscious decision making about which coaching format will be the best fit for a particular teacher or group of teachers. From the array of tools the continuum offers, the coach and teachers must deliberately select *the right tool for the job*. Articulating a specific format of professional learning enables coaches to design evaluation schemes to measure effectiveness and raises their awareness of the personal and professional needs of the staff members they are working with.

The Literacy Coaching Continuum also allows for various points of entry for individual teachers, depending on their needs, skill level, and identified professional learning goals. The model assumes that a trusting relationship exists between the teacher and the coach, and that they collaborate in making any decisions regarding the best match between the need and the coaching format chosen. For example, a teacher who is being introduced to a new practice might feel that it is best to begin with resource management, content presentations, and focused classroom visits, so that he can become comfortable with the practice, understand the rationale for it, and see the practice implemented with fidelity.

Finally, the Literacy Coaching Continuum makes it possible for one coach to facilitate a range of learning opportunities for teachers, because not all of the formats require hands-on support from the coach on a daily basis. Let's consider what this differentiated approach might look like if text comprehension were the content focus:

• The coach initiates two *study groups* and then turns leadership over to the teachers. Group 1 studies the book *Strategies That Work* (Harvey & Goudvis, 2000). Group 2 works on a scheme to evaluate instruction on a strategy for text comprehension.

• The coach gives a *content presentation* on the teaching of a text comprehension strategy (questioning). The presentation and demonstration are videotaped for teachers who are not at the meeting, or for review by those who are. The coach walks the teachers through the process of gradual release of responsibility:

   – Explicit description of the strategy (when and how it should be used).
   – Teacher or student modeling of the strategy in action.
   – Collaborative use of the strategy in action.
   – Guided practice.
   – Independent use.

• The coach gives *demonstration lessons* of the text comprehension strategy (questioning).

• The coach works with three teachers on *collaborative resource management* (choosing texts for comprehension strategy instruction, making classroom charts on these strategies). After the first meeting, the teachers take on the task. At a staff meeting, the teachers will share the lists of books they have generated for strategy instruction and give each teacher a set of strategy posters.

• Five teachers plan a *focused classroom visit* to the classroom of a teacher at a neighboring school who has implemented instruction in the strategy for two years.

• Some teachers are *coplanning* a series of lessons to align writing instruction with language arts. They invite the coach to *coteach* a lesson. This lesson will be videotaped for later review by the team. The focus question is "How do the strategies support writing instruction?"

• *Peer coaching* takes place in classrooms where teachers are trying out instruction on the strategy for text comprehension.

Obviously, this well-oiled differentiation is atypical in the initial days of implementation, but rest assured that it can happen. I've heard many coaches just getting a program under way lament that teachers weren't using their services, only to hear, a year later, that they can't keep up with the requests for collaboration.

This is a good time to point out that the coaching formats of the continuum are offered as tools to be selected judiciously. I'm not challenging any literacy coach to juggle all of the formats at once; rather, I hope that literacy coaches and the teachers and school leaders with whom they work will engage in discussions about the best "fit" for the professional learning needs that have emerged from a thorough review of student data. Less is often more than enough.

The Importance of Good Communication

Communication plays a major role in coaching. Although the role of the coach may shift according to the format used, communication skills are always the underpinning of an effective working relationship between the coach and the teachers. Whether the coach is facilitating a study group, demonstrating a lesson, or observing a teacher's practice, the hallmark of the interaction is the communication skills that the coach and the teachers bring to the table. To echo Wellman and Lipton (2004), this set of skills includes building and maintaining trust, pausing and paraphrasing, conscious use of thoughtful questions, presuming positive presuppositions, and pursuing a balance between advocacy and inquiry. Among the many other books on communication skills that are useful for literacy coaches beginning new programs (or interested in enhancing existing ones), there are two I recommend particularly: *Instructional Coaching: A Partnership Approach to Improving Instruction* (2007) by M. James Knight, and *Literacy Coaching: Developing Effective Teachers Through Instructional Dialogue* (2006) by Marilyn Duncan.

In the chapters that follow, I explore the research base for coaching, describe the various facets of the Literacy Coaching Continuum, and offer professional learning tools and activities that can prepare and sustain literacy coaches in their challenging role.

One for All and All for One!

In April 2007, I was fortunate to spend a few days at W. H. Horton School in Newark, New Jersey. There, I had the pleasure of meeting with the literacy coach, math coach, inclusion specialist, and lead science teacher. Their collaborative partnership, supported by a very able administrative team, highlighted the positive power of a respectful and focused coaching program.

The team focuses on common goals and objectives (comprehension strategy instruction) that are linked to learning standards. They recognize and celebrate strengths, while offering alternative approaches to meeting the challenges of teaching. They exemplify the proactive stance that "we are in this together" and, as a consequence, actively model and encourage creative problem solving and self-reflection through a variety of structured learning opportunities (vertical and horizontal team meetings to share content information, review lessons, and analyze student data were a few formats that I observed during my visit).

I observed teachers reporting examples of their own implementation of comprehension strategy lessons, sharing data on student impact, and discussing modification they might make to improve their instruction. It was a striking reminder of the benefits of a thoughtful, consistent, and inclusive coaching program.

In the following vignette, you will read a detailed description of one coach's rendition of "a thoughtful, consistent, and inclusive coaching program." Standing "on the balcony" on a regular basis can help literacy coaches get a clear and comprehensive view of their own professional learning efforts. If you are a literacy coach, consider writing your own coaching story as a way to help you gather your own evidence of collaboration.

One Teacher at a Time

by John Moran, Literacy Facilitator, Irwin Avenue Elementary School
Charlotte, North Carolina

As a literacy facilitator at an elementary school in a large urban school district, I sometimes face a daunting task. Judy Fahl, my building administrator, likes to say that change occurs by working with one teacher at a time. With

that in mind, I believe that it isn't one format of coaching that works best, but a combination of the following:

- *Professional development workshops centered on a common vision.*
- *Observation by the literacy coach of the classroom teacher.*
- *Direct consultation with the individual teacher to review strengths and needs, and then outlining a course of action of steps to be taken, from my perspective, for refining classroom practice.*
- *Demonstrating the techniques previously outlined with the children as the teacher observes.*
- *Reflective consultative conversation with the individual teacher to debrief on the implementation of the literacy engagements.*
- *The development of literacy engagements collaboratively centered on the agreed-upon goals.*
- *Implementation of the lesson by the classroom teacher while the literacy coach observes.*
- *Postconsultative conversation with the individual teacher to reflect on the delivery of the lesson, provide feedback, and create a time line for sustained growth.*

At the school where I am the literacy facilitator, professional development opportunities are provided for teachers, literacy tutors, and other support personnel over the course of the school year so that all of us have a common thread of experience. During the last four years, I have used this model of literacy coaching with varying degrees of success with both seasoned veterans and teachers in their first years as professionals. The individual steps taken vary depending on the direction that each teacher wishes to take.

Lindsay Fries, a 2nd grade teacher in her first years of teaching, requested additional support as she implemented small-group guided reading engagements for her students. I asked her what she felt she was doing well before we talked about what she needed in order to grow as a teacher.

Lindsay felt that she had the classroom management aspect of her teaching down, with students working in centers as she met with individual groups, and she was pretty sure that the students were appropriately grouped based on the

available data. Having observed her teaching on numerous occasions, I agreed. Lindsay then went on to say that the structure and content of the small-group instructional focus needed to be strengthened, based on her own reflection as well as a formative observation by the building administrator. Together, we mapped out a time line that included the selection of appropriate texts for her groupings and times when I could demonstrate the structure of small-group instructional guided reading groups, as well as provide a lesson plan format for teaching directly the skills and strategies that each text provided.

The next step was the actual instructional implementation within the small group, with Lindsay by my side. I explained to the students that I would stop periodically and explain to their teacher what I was doing; in much the same way that they were learners, we teachers continue to learn as well.

This "adult teaching time" in the act of instruction opens the door for questions based on what unfolds and, from my perspective, is extremely important for further inquiry into teacher-generated learning. After these guided demonstration lessons, follow-up via ongoing conversations, collaborative planning sessions, and continued support are needed for sustained growth of teachers' curricular development over time.

2

Is There a Research Base That Supports Coaching?

For a number of years, I have been following coaching efforts in the United Kingdom, particularly the work of the National College for School Leadership (NCSL), which provides professional development opportunities and support for school leaders as both individuals and members of teams. One of the issues that NCSL studies and disseminates information on is how to advance teachers' active engagement in the realm of research.

Cordingley and Bell (2002) discuss the position of "school research coordinator," whose function is to "act as [an agent] of change, motivating, assessing and organizing teachers' engagement in and with research and expanding teacher discussion of pedagogy" (p. 5). Although the authors are not talking about literacy coaches specifically, their characterization provides an appropriate description of a preeminent role of the literacy coach and touches on an intrinsic component of the job's responsibility. This belief is infused into the Literacy Coaching Continuum.

Research and Practice: An Unbalanced Equation

Sharon Walpole (2004) calls literacy coaching "a practice in search of research" (p. 1). We educators find ourselves in an interesting albeit contradictory situation. Despite the current emphasis on scientifically based research, few substantive studies are available to guide practitioners on the key issues of literacy coaching, which include the following:

- Optimal number of coaches of teachers to students.
- Essential elements of effective practice (skills, knowledge, schedules, formats).
- Importance of clarity in the roles of the coach and the teachers in the process.
- Kinds of professional development (initial and ongoing) that support the implementation.
- Essential attributes of personnel assigned as coaches.
- Importance and level of interface with other professional development initiatives.
- Methods for measuring success for coach, teachers, and students.
- Issues of supervision and support (initial and ongoing).

The contradiction is that despite the relatively little empirical evidence that supports coaching (and its link to student achievement), policies and practices for coaching are being put in place on a massive scale. For example, the No Child Left Behind Act of 2001 stipulates that states must make available to new and veteran teachers and principals "teacher mentoring, team teaching, reduced class schedules, and intensive professional development and use standards or assessments for guiding beginning teachers that are consistent with challenging State student academic achievement standards and with the requirements for professional development activities described in section 9101" (Sec. 2113.c.2).

In the document *Guidance for the Reading First Program* (U.S. Department of Education, 2002), "coaches, mentors, peers, and outside experts" are advised "to develop and implement practices and strategies for professional development that should be evident in an effective reading program" (p. 7). Professional development must be an "ongoing, continuous activity, and not consist of 'one-shot' workshops or lectures. Delivery mechanisms should include the use of coaches and other teachers of reading who provide feedback as instructional strategies are put into practice" (p. 26).

Like policymakers, leaders in the field are also promoting the use of coaches. In *Teaching Reading IS Rocket Science*, Louisa C. Moats (1999) promotes high-quality professional development for teachers that includes the use of "in-class" coaches:

> Every teacher who currently teaches reading would benefit from high-quality education about reading development, language structure, and recent research findings. Validated instructional programs should be accessible to every teacher, along with

consultation and demonstration of their effective use. Teachers need ongoing professional development that has topical continuity, practical application, and opportunities for collaboration with peers. These professional development experiences should be linked to continuous in-class coaching. (p. 25)

In 2000, the Learning First Alliance published a report titled *Every Child Reading: A Professional Development Guide.* This report acknowledges that teaching requires a vast array of skills and astute judgment about *when to use what, with whom, and why.* Coaching is presented as an important component of the professional development that must be provided to teachers as they learn new skills and seek to infuse the latest knowledge into their daily practice.

Moreover, a number of organizations that seek to develop teacher quality—including the National Staff Development Council (NSDC), the National Council of Teachers of English (NCTE), and the International Reading Association (IRA)—provide information and support to schools, districts, and states that want to implement quality coaching programs.

Given all this interest in and support for the role of coaching in professional development, should literacy coaches suspend their practice (if they could) and wait for the research to catch up? Think about this question while I share my thoughts with you.

For three consecutive years, starting in 2002, I attended national invitational Focus Forums on scientifically based reading research sponsored by the Pacific Regional Educational Laboratory. Well-respected researchers in the field of literacy were invited to present recent work to a relatively small group of practitioners, including teachers and professional development providers.

Over the course of three years, we received updates on research related to text comprehension, fluency, and vocabulary. Each forum was invigorating and exciting, but also somewhat discouraging. Each time, I was reminded of the great divide that separates research and practice, and I felt sorry that more teachers were not taking part in the exchange. The good news is that the Focus Forum publication and presentation materials are available online at www.prel.org/programs/rel/rel.asp, including those from the forum held in 2005 on the topic of professional development.

At about the same time as the first forum, I came across an article in *Educational Researcher* titled "A Knowledge Base for the Teaching Profession: What Would It Look Like and How Can We Get One?" (Hiebert et al., 2002). The authors propose that to improve classroom teaching in a systemic and sustained way, the teaching profession needs a knowledge base that also grows and improves. They point out that "in spite of the continuing efforts of researchers, archived research knowledge has had little effect on the improvement of practice in the average classroom" (p. 3). The problem isn't that teachers aren't gathering a lot of their own data, but that traditional research knowledge and practitioners' experience-based knowledge rarely meet in the middle to inform and improve practice. It was heartening to see my own questions and concerns addressed so succinctly in an article, especially when the authors also proposed some possible solutions to this age-old dilemma of how to transform practitioner knowledge into professional knowledge.

Hiebert and colleagues (2002) also note that practitioner knowledge, or "craft knowledge," is distinctively linked to classroom practice. It develops in response to particular problems of practice and is grounded in the context in which teachers (and literacy coaches) work. Craft knowledge tends to be detailed, concrete, and specific. On the other hand, *professional knowledge* (1) must be public; (2) must be storable and shareable; and (3) must have a mechanism for verification and improvement.

A prime example of turning practitioner knowledge into professional knowledge is the process called *lesson study,* which originated in Japan. In this process, small groups of teachers meet regularly to design, implement, observe, evaluate, and modify lessons. Each yearlong study cycle involves testing hypotheses, verifying teacher knowledge (what we think and how it can be generalized to all lessons), and observing gains in student learning. Results of successful lessons are shared publicly via staff meetings, lesson study networks, and directories.

Moving to Professional Knowledge

Let's go back to my earlier question. Given all this interest in and support for the role of coaching in professional learning, should literacy coaches suspend their practice and wait for the research to catch up? Absolutely not!

The caveat, I believe, is that coaches need to continue to explore the promising role of coaching by actively incorporating the strategies advocated by Hiebert and colleagues into their work so that practitioner knowledge can become professional knowledge. Coaches need to acknowledge, learn from, and disseminate information about current efforts. They also need to articulate what form their professional learning will take (choosing from the formats in the Literacy Coaching Continuum) and design evaluation procedures that measure adult learning, change in practice, and subsequent increases in student performance so as to verify effectiveness.

Snow and colleagues (2005) refer to this process as "a recurrent cycle of learning, enactment, assessment, and reflection" (p. 2). They contend that lack of a "fully specified research base" should not discourage coaches "regarding the value of what [they] do know or the appropriateness of much current practice in teacher education." The key is to be well informed and current in the knowledge of teacher professional development, student learning, and literacy. Literacy coaches need to be supported in their efforts to read, reflect on, apply, and evaluate the application of pertinent research.

Gersten, Vaughn, Deschler, and Schiller (1997) identify six guiding principles that must be attended to if teachers are to make use of research in their classroom practice:

- *Reality principle*—Is the practice feasible?
- *Scope*—Is the scale reasonable? If the scope is too broad, teachers will feel overwhelmed. If it's too narrow, teachers will wonder if it's worth their time and effort to engage in the practice.
- *Technical aspects*—Are the teachers receiving adequate support and feedback to inform their practice?
- *Conceptual aspects*—Do the teachers understand the significance of the new practice?
- *Linkages*—Are the connections to other initiatives transparent?
- *Collegial support networks*—Are there supports in place to sustain innovations?

Examples from the Field

Let's look at a few examples of how coaching programs are observing, testing, and replicating promising practices that marry the expertise and unique skills of teachers and researchers.

In 2004, the Saginaw Bay Writing Project and the Saginaw Valley State University in Michigan published a monograph that reviewed literacy study groups from their inception in 1996 through their expansion in 1999–2001. The participants and researchers believe that the study groups were instrumental in a slow but impressive increase in scores on the Michigan Educational Assessment Program from 1995 to 2001. The report (Weaver, Rentsch, & Calliari, 2004) outlines the researchers' methodology for data collection and showcases the forms they used to gather information.

The South Carolina Reading Initiative (SCRI) is designed to broaden and deepen teachers' understanding of the reading process and the professional literature. A report from the initiative (DeFord et al., 2003) looks at a specific instructional practice (strategy instruction) that was a focus of the coaching interactions. The researchers collected and analyzed data that linked the use and fidelity of the practice (supported by professional development) to student learning (in this case, increased use of cueing strategies). After only one year of SCRI instruction (taught by teachers who received professional development on using assessment to inform instruction and teaching for strategies), significant differences in students' use of strategies were noted.

The purpose of the Hillsborough County Public Schools' Coaching Program in Tampa, Florida, is to provide support to primary teachers to improve instructional practice so as to increase student achievement. In October 2003, program participants issued a follow-up report (Albritton, 2003) to review student achievement data, participant coaches' reactions, and questions that remained unanswered. The concerns and issues identified were used to generate a list of recommendations to guide their future work.

For a number of years, the Center for Research on Learning at the University of Kansas has been conducting research on its Instructional Coaching Model under the direction of Jim Knight. The coaching model was developed to support teachers as they implement the Strategy Instruction Model (SIM) techniques in the classroom. According to information posted on the project Web site (www.instructionalcoach. org/research.html), the research focuses on three questions: (1) Does coaching lead to implementation? (2) What about fidelity? (3) What do teachers think about coaching? Knight (2007) found that coaching "does lead to successful adoption and effective use of proven instructional methods, with one crucial caveat": the coaching program must have strong administrative support and qualified coaches (p.1).

The *2005 Evaluation of the Alabama Reading Initiative* (ARI) by Edward Moscovitch (2006) of Cape Ann Economics summarizes the data that have been collected over the course of this statewide project showing a dramatic improvement in the reading proficiency of primary grade students. The author attributes the gain largely to the ARI principal coaches—instructional leaders, identified as "outstanding," who provide support to their peers—and trainers of reading coaches. He recommends that additional trainers of reading coaches be hired to "spend more time in schools, working on-site with school-based reading coaches and/or modeling and coaching alongside the principal coaches" (p. 15).

Literacy coaches might want to share these and other research documents with teachers to spark a discussion on the importance of having a focus for coaching, how data can inform subsequent practice, potential methodology and tools for data collection, prospective reporting formats, and collaboration with universities.

A Large-Scale Study of Coaching

On the national front, a large-scale, federally funded research project is expected to provide valuable insights about some aspects of coaching. The Professional Development in Reading Study is evaluating the impact of two professional development approaches. Model 1 is the typical weeklong summer institute followed by three one-day seminars during the regular school year. Model 2 adds in-school coaching to the mix. The study, which began with a pilot during the 2004–2005 school year and is scheduled for completion in 2008, is examining both teacher practice and student achievement. The study focuses on 2nd grade teachers who are already using either *Open Court Reading* or Houghton Mifflin's *Legacy of Literacy/Nation's Choice*.

Research questions being addressed in this study are the following:

• What effects do summer institutes with scientifically based content and modest follow-up during the school year (Model 1) have on teacher knowledge, instructional practices, and student reading achievement? What is the incremental effect of adding in-school coaching to these services (Model 2)?

• To what extent are the effects of the two treatment models on student reading achievement mediated by the models' effects on teacher knowledge and instructional practice?

• To what extent do the effects of the two treatment models depend on the reading program being implemented in the district, the characteristics of students being served by the schools, or the prior knowledge or other characteristics of teachers?

• How do the effects of the two treatment models change over time? Do the effects of the models on teacher knowledge and instruction grow, stabilize, or fade over the course of the study period?

• To what extent do the effects of the two treatment models vary according to the amount of professional development received by the teachers at each school?

• What are the per-teacher costs of participating in the two treatment models?

Additional information about the study is available at www.mdrc.org/project_28_67.html.

A Literacy Coaching Clearinghouse

In 2006, the International Reading Association and the National Council of Teachers of English launched a joint effort called the Literacy Coaching Clearinghouse (LCC). The clearinghouse, located at the University of Colorado at Denver and Health Sciences Center, is designed to provide educators with information about factors that contribute to the success of literacy programs in the United States. The LCC's Web site (www. literacycoachingonline.org/) offers a variety of resources and ways to contribute to the exchange of knowledge. One example of the resources available is a document titled *Qualifications for Literacy Coaches: Achieving the Gold Standard* by Sharon Frost and Rita Bean. In line with the recommendations of Hiebert and colleagues (2002), the clearinghouse has the potential to help transform practitioner knowledge into professional knowledge by making information about literacy coaching *public, storable,* and *shareable,* thereby contributing to the promise of *verification and improvement of practice*.

Measuring Effectiveness

A concern for anyone who is incorporating coaching into professional development plans is how to initiate and sustain *local efforts* to measure effectiveness. Thomas Guskey (2000) provides a thoughtful framework for evaluating the impact of professional development (see Figure 2.1). He recommends planning with the "end in mind" (Level 5—Student Learning Outcomes), working backward through each successive level. In designing and planning learning opportunities, keep in mind how you will measure outcomes. All too often, we wait until the end of the initiative before we begin to figure out how we will evaluate our efforts.

Joellen Killion (2003), director of special projects at the National Staff Development Council, suggests an eight-step process for evaluating the impact of professional development. The first step is to *assess evaluability*. Simply put, this means that if you can't figure out how to evaluate your program, then you should rethink your plan. Notice that the first step precedes any instructional action. This is important. Don't wait until you're knee-deep in the innovation before you start to assess its value.

After determining that impact can be measured, it's time for the second step: *formulate evaluation questions*. These questions should include formative (initial and ongoing) and summative (final) questions. Killion suggests that evaluation questions should focus on the results rather than the services, so that impact rather than program delivery is measured.

Figure 2.1   Guskey's Five Levels of Evaluation

---

1. Participants' Reactions

Evaluation at this level recognizes that "measuring participants' initial satisfaction with the experience can help . . . improve the design and delivery of programs or activities in valid ways." This can be accomplished by asking questions such as these:

- Did the teachers think their time was well spent?
- Were the activities meaningful?
- Did teachers think the activities would be useful in practice?

2. Participants' Learning

Evaluation at this level "focuses on measuring the knowledge and skills that participants gained." Ways to measure these include the following:

- Pencil-and-paper exercises.
- Simulation or skill demonstrations.
- Oral or written personal reflections.
- Portfolio evaluation or similar activities.

3. Organization Support and Change

Evaluation at this level is meant to determine if "organization policies . . . undermine implementation efforts" or support them. Appropriate questions to ask include the following:

- Was individual change encouraged and supported?
- Was administrative support public and overt?
- Were problems addressed quickly and efficiently?
- Were sufficient resources made available, including time for sharing and reflection?
- Were successes recognized and shared?

4. Participants' Use of New Knowledge and Skills

The focus of evaluation at this level is whether or not "new knowledge and skills that participants learned make a difference in their professional practice." An ongoing review of the degree and quality of use of new knowledge and skills can be accomplished through the following vehicles:

- Questionnaires or structured interviews.
- Oral or written personal reflections.
- Examination of journals or portfolios.
- Direct observation or observation via video or audio recording.

5. Student Learning Outcomes

Evaluation at this level seeks to determine the effect on student learning from a professional development experience. Questions to ask may include the following:

- Did students show improvement in academic achievement, behavior, or other areas?
- Did the students benefit from the activity?
- Were there any unintended results?

Source: From "Does It Make a Difference? Evaluating Professional Development," by T. R. Guskey, 2002, *Educational Leadership, 59*(3), pp. 45–51. Copyright © 2002 by T. R. Guskey. Adapted with permission.

The third step is to *construct the evaluation framework,* which includes making decisions about what evidence to collect, from whom or what sources, collection mechanisms, and subsequent analysis of the information. You are then ready for the fourth through seventh steps: *collect data, organize and analyze data, interpret data,* and *disseminate findings.* Last, you should *evaluate the evaluation* to consider whether or not the process met or exceeded your goals and to provide valuable insights to inform future practices.

📁 Professional Learning

For suggestions on engaging literacy coaches in a discussion of how to use the Guskey and Killion protocols to assess practice, see Part III's **Module 11: Evaluating Professional Learning: Exploring Points of View.**

Questions for Discussion

1. The article by Hiebert, Gallimore, and Stigler (2002) focuses on the professional development of teachers. Do you think that the issues explored in this article also apply to the professional development and support of literacy coaches? If so, why?

2. Can you think of national professional development initiatives that are attempting to transform practitioner knowledge into professional knowledge? Share your perspective on why they fit the bill.

3. What can you do locally to transform practitioner knowledge into professional knowledge?

4. Neufeld and Roper (2003) view coaching as a "natural outgrowth of the lessons cognitive psychology has taught us about what it means to learn and to know something" (p. 10). This comment resonates with me. I view my own learning journey as a progressive and continual tableau of engagement, inquiry, and experimentation. What do you think? Do you agree with Neufield and Roper? Why or why not?

5. In looking over Guskey's Five Levels of Evaluation (Figure 2.1), what are some examples of how you currently collect data at each tier?

6. Having developed a plan for evaluating your professional development efforts, how will you communicate the results to your colleagues and community?

PART II

The Components of the
LITERACY COACHING
CONTINUUM

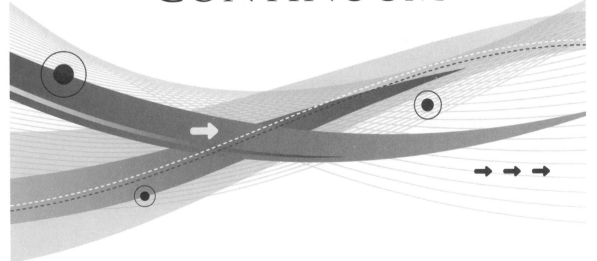

3

Collaborative Resource Management

Collaborative resource management anchors one end of the Literacy Coaching Continuum. In this learning format, the literacy coach works with teachers to help them become familiar with available resources. The focus should be on the review and management of materials and teaching resources that are directly related to the focus and objectives of the coaching. The coach can also help the teacher manage the instructional assets in a thoughtful and proactive way. Professional learning interactions centered on "stuff" can provide many opportunities for rich conversation about the heart of teaching: students and the instructional plan to meet their needs.

The Coach's Role

In their work in collaborative resource management, coaches might be expected to do the following:

- Effectively use resources as necessary.
- Share knowledge of successful techniques in classroom management and instructional planning for effective literacy instruction.
- Assist teachers with the appropriate use of core and supplemental instructional materials that align with district and state curriculums.
- Help teachers select books and other instructional materials to meet individual literacy needs.

- Examine, evaluate, and recommend instructional methods, materials, and equipment, including technology.
- Maintain a bookroom or similar collection of resources for use in guided reading groups and other literacy strategies.
- Help set up a classroom environment that is conducive to effective literacy instruction (e.g., with centers, a classroom library, and bulletin boards at children's eye level for posting work).
- Identify needs and make recommendations for appropriate reading and writing intervention materials.
- Coordinate the inventory, ordering, and distribution of leveled texts.
- Use available guidance to review core, supplemental, and intensive intervention materials under consideration for purchase, looking for evidence that the materials are aligned with federal program requirements, such as those of Reading First.

Note that these job activities highlight *helping to choose appropriate instructional resources* as well as *facilitating the organization and effective integration of the materials.*

The Importance of Resource Management

Is it any wonder that collaborative resource management is an important scaffold in professional learning? In college we learn about curriculum and teaching materials from our professors. Their choices are, as one would expect, guided by their particular philosophy, and so we tend to see only a limited representation of the full range of available resources. When we get our first teaching job, we often inherit a cache of instructional supplies from the person who preceded us. Sometimes the materials are carefully stored and inventoried; more often they are not. We may be familiar with the "stuff"; more often we are not. At the other extreme is the teacher who is just starting out in the profession or at the site, in a new classroom, with a limited budget and not much inventory to start with. Sometimes we are told what core curriculum materials we must use without having been part of the decision-making process. Sometimes we were part of the decision-making process but disagreed with the decision. Both scenarios present resource management challenges that teachers must face and adapt to in the course of their teaching careers.

As soon as new teachers enter the classroom, they are bombarded with information about the "latest and greatest" programs that are "scientifically based" and ready to roll out for success. Open any professional journal and ads for "research-based" materials jump off the pages with promised solutions to instructional challenges. What to buy, why to buy it, and for whom it will be most effective are questions that teachers must grapple with. Becoming an informed consumer is an important aspect of effective teaching. Helping our peers become informed consumers is an important aspect of effective coaching.

Richard L. Allington (2005) suggests that there are three issues to attend to when reviewing the application of commercial materials to instructional practice. Educators must first reflect on the evidence that "using the product develops teachers' expertise about effective reading instruction" (p. 16). Given that teacher expertise is a critical feature of effective literacy instruction, we would be ill-advised, Allington points out, to choose products that hold little promise for increasing teacher knowledge. Reviewing materials through this lens encourages us to judge the comprehensiveness of the support materials and to question whether the materials are aligned with research and best practice. Unfortunately, this perspective on resource acquisition is rare. Educators are much more likely to focus on how we will apply the resources to help our students than we are to think about how the resources will affect our skill and knowledge growth.

What would a product look like that developed teachers' expertise about effective reading instruction? I'll take a crack at this question, and I recommend that you do the same. Commercial materials that develop teachers' expertise about effective reading instruction exhibit the following qualities:

• They are organized around research-based principles regarding what children need in order to learn to read and to read to learn.

• They provide detailed information to the teacher on the rationale for the program content (scope, assessment/instruction cycle) and organization (sequence, pacing).

• They are explicit about, and provide models of, exemplary practices in their format and content—that is, they are culturally responsive, provide universal access, are motivational, tap into students' funds of knowledge, and provide opportunities for active engagement by students.

• They are sensitive to the needs and skills of teachers at various points in their career.

A second consideration that Allington suggests is the "role you intend the product to play in the total literacy curriculum" (p. 16). This suggestion reminds us that no one commercial product by itself can provide a complete program. We must be thoughtful and selective in our choices, so that we don't end up with a multilayered curriculum hodgepodge. Sharon Walpole and Michael C. McKenna (2004) warn us that some teachers, "mindful of the pendulum swings that they have experienced, cling to their old materials and create a hybrid program that combines elements of their old materials with elements of the new ones. [Be] proactive in preventing this practice, which is known as layering" (p. 155). I echo that cautionary note. I have worked with teachers who have patched together a literacy program that would delight an archeologist. The "layers" tell a tale of fickle interventions and faddish responses to long-term challenges.

Last, Allington (2005) says we need to consider the "interest level of the product and its potential to engage minds and foster an interest in reading" (p. 16). We know that student engagement is an essential feature of reading achievement (Guthrie, Wigfield, & Perencevich, 2004). Leaving this critical element out of the mix is a recipe for failure. Asking students what they find motivating and interesting is an essential component of an instructional materials review.

Choosing Materials to Support Instruction

My first teaching job was as a special educator in northern Vermont. My class was newly established to meet the needs of a small group of students who had recently been deinstitutionalized and placed in a local foster-care home. My students ranged in age from 7 to 12 and came with the labels *autistic* and *developmentally delayed*. Labels, as you know, do not give a teacher much to go on.

My classroom had no supplies because the program was brand new—a clean slate, so to speak. As a consequence, I didn't begin my teaching career connecting instruction with any specific materials. Fortunately, I had an instructional coach who stressed that teaching was about getting to know my students, observing their current status, and planning instruction to move them forward. She guided me as I made decisions about what materials to buy to *support* my instructional plans.

In my first year of teaching, I never did buy the packaged curriculum materials that made teaching seem so neat and tidy. With the help of my coach and more experienced peers, I chose support items that my students would gravitate to in a meaningful way. In hindsight I know that even with the best materials on hand, teaching is not neat and tidy. However, selecting appropriate curriculum materials and using them with fidelity goes a long way toward making the job more manageable.

Linda Darling-Hammond (2003) reports that in 2000, new teachers who received training in specific facets of teaching, participated in practice teaching, and received feedback on their teaching were less likely by half to leave the teaching profession. One aspect of the training provided was the selection and use of instructional materials.

In a report titled *Resources, Instruction, and Research*, Cohen, Raudenbush, and Ball (2000) from the Center for the Study of Teaching and Policy explore this question: *What resources matter, how, and under what circumstances?* The underpinning for this working paper is that instruction is not simply what teachers do; it is the "interactions among teachers, students, and content, in environments" (p. 10). The authors point out that a "well-articulated regime ought to be clear about the required resources and justify the claim by exploring how resources are used to achieve specific aims" (p. 27). They also suggest that it is important to shift the conversation from conventional instructional resources in the abstract to how the resources build on and enhance well-grounded learning goals.

The Ohio Department of Education (2006) has instituted a Literacy Specialist Endorsement that is valid for "providing coaching and professional development in the teaching of reading for classroom teachers at all grade levels" (p. 1). Their *Standards Matrix* articulates the categories and indicators of the foundational knowledge for the endorsement. Under the category of "Curriculum, Instructional Strategies, and Materials," the matrix states: "Candidates have knowledge of a wide range of instructional practices, approaches, methods, and curriculum materials to support reading and writing instruction" (p. 5). The indicators for the endorsement include the following elements:

- Effectively use a variety of curriculum materials including technology-based materials to assist teachers in planning multilevel instruction.
- Plan and provide professional development programs that increase the knowledge base for teachers, professionals, parents, and administrators in the use of curriculum materials.
- Coach teachers in the use of a wide range of print and nonprint materials, including technology-based materials.
- Evaluate specific curriculum materials according to evidence-based research that supports the different practices.
- Compare and contrast, use, interpret, and recommend a wide range of assessment tools and practices.
- Provide professional development to teachers in the selection of books, technology-based information, and non-print materials representing multiple levels, broad interests, reading abilities, cultural and linguistic backgrounds. (Ohio Department of Education, 2006, pp. 5–7)

Clearly, the Ohio Department of Education considers collaborative resource management an important aspect of the job of the literacy coach. I agree.

Getting Started

So where do you start with collaborative resource management? In my work as a literacy coach, I have found it helpful to begin by facilitating a thorough review of the resources on hand. This review simply requires that a group of teachers works together to inventory the curriculum, assessment, and human resources that they currently have access to.

📁 Professional Learning

For suggested materials, procedures, and guiding questions for the inventory process, see Part III's **Module 7: Literacy Program Inventory**. This three-part module, focused on assessments, instructional materials, and human resources, emerged from work with a group of teachers who complained that they had so many instructional programs available to them that they didn't know where to start.

A literacy program inventory can help a coach do the following:

• Identify gaps. For example, teachers might discover that they are spending a tremendous amount of time on phonics instruction and that fluency is being ignored.

• Determine areas of overlap. This combats the "silver bullet" approach—a situation in which so many instructional packages are available in the school that the teachers are confused about what to use, when to use it, and with whom.

• Talk about resources. This helps to spark rich conversations about students and their instructional needs.

• Put the role of resources into proper perspective. Instructional tools shouldn't define the job to be done, but they should provide support in pursuit of the learning goal.

• Review human resources to enable planning for better collaboration. For example, in one school district, this process led to improved communication and service alignment between consultants, district literacy coaches, and the inclusion support staff.

• Recall that instructional materials have an intended purpose and that we need to be careful not to overuse or misuse the resources.

- Remember that instruction should be aligned to learning standards.
- Encourage cross-conversation among content teachers.

Another helpful tactic is to coordinate and collaborate for coherence by inviting various partners to the table to bring clarity to the task at hand. For example, when a colleague and I worked with literacy coaches at a district in Ohio, we would sometimes co-present at our network meetings with Sharon Martin, a representative from Scholastic Press whose reading series (*The Literacy Place*) was being used by the district. This helped us eliminate some of the fragmentation and confusion that can result when multiple parties approach common issues from different perspectives. For example, at one session on the topic of text comprehension strategies, Sharon shared some of *The Literacy Place* assessments that would be useful in measuring student gain in comprehension, while we demonstrated some potential teaching tools for strategy instruction. This type of coordination is one way to work smarter instead of harder.

In this same spirit of collaboration, a literacy coach might invite the library media specialists, technology support personnel, special education and content teachers, and others to regular team meetings. Two questions that should be on the table at each meeting are "Who else should be here to inform and enhance the work we are about to do?" and "Who else will have valuable information regarding appropriate instructional resources?"

Effective Use of Instructional Materials

In the study *Learning to Read—Lessons from Exemplary First-Grade Classrooms* (Pressley, Allington, Wharton-McDonald, Block, & Morrow, 2001), the authors note that high-achieving classrooms were also well-managed classrooms, with teachers following regular but flexible routines, planning in advance, and effectively managing both time and other adults in the classroom. Charlotte Danielson (1996) includes "management of materials and supplies" as an important component of the classroom environment and describes "distinguished" teachers as having "seamless" routines for handling materials and supplies, "with students assuming some responsibility for efficient operation" (p. 84). She also considers the organization of physical space—including making all learning equally accessible to all students—an essential element of effective teaching. The points these authors make about the importance of management and organization are worth our attention.

I consider myself an organized person. I rarely tackle an assignment without carefully choosing materials that I might need and tidying up my area so that I can focus on the task at hand. This physical order helps me organize mentally as well. I'm not obsessive about tidiness, but the dipstick test for me is this: Do I have the right tools for the job easily accessible so there's no need to plow through a bunch of extraneous items? If I don't, the outcome is an inability to focus and get things done. When I'm teaching, the dipstick test must also include the impact of my organization on the students (adults or children) I'm working with.

On one of my assignments a few years ago, I was visiting a kindergarten classroom. The teacher, Mrs. K., indicated that she needed support with behavior management issues and asked me to help her "bring order to the chaos of her classroom." It was a delight to observe Mrs. K. interacting with her children: she was respectful, enthusiastic, and creative. The problem was that she often had to stop her instruction to locate materials before she could proceed. At one point, she asked to me to head over to the literacy centers she had established. Had I not known what to look for, it would have been easy to miss them, as they were hidden among stacks of unrelated paperwork and sundry storage items. It's hard to direct children to follow a routine, such as going to the literacy centers, when they can't *find* the location where the routine should take place.

My first reaction to the chaos was to pitch in and help Mrs. K. clean up the classroom. (Organized people love to organize other people!) My fingers were itching to activate the broom brigade, but apparently several of her colleagues had already tried this intervention, and, as she put it, "it didn't take." Short-term solutions, although satisfying at the moment, don't necessarily influence practice in the future. The neat classroom doesn't necessarily remain tidy! Instead, Mrs. K. and I began focused conversations about her request. What did she want, why did she want it, and what did she have to do to get there? She talked about how her disorganization disrupted her teaching routine and how these disruptions affected her students. This was the hook that snagged her. She started to pay careful attention and to discern the *real* reason for interruptions in learning. When she had to pause during a lesson to find something, her students became restless, unfocused, and distractible. She realized that what she had initially pegged as a behavior management issue was in fact the children's reaction to *her* lack of organizational planning.

I am reminded of the sentiment expressed by Arthur L. Costa and Robert J. Garmston in the video training series *Another Set of Eyes* (1988). They note that

The coach is not interested in creating the perfect lesson, but in exercising and enhancing the thinking that goes on behind the teacher's actions. Coaches ask questions and give responses that are designed to encourage, clarify, and probe so as to discover the thinking behind the teacher's decisions.

Examples from the Field

The specific tasks related to collaborative resource management will vary, of course, depending on program objectives, staff needs, and other considerations. To get an idea of typical tasks, let's look at some examples of resource management activities taken from the six-week reports that literacy coaches in a district in Ohio submitted to their principals:

* Distributed and reviewed materials for the Extended Learning Opportunity program (an after-school program).
* Worked with a teacher to complete a nonfiction book order.
* Helped teachers to bag and label nonfiction guided-reading books.
* Helped teachers to organize books in the book room.
* Copied and distributed running records, phonemic awareness assessments, and class lists for grades K–3.
* Met with a teacher to discuss phonics instruction and reviewed some curriculum resources with her.
* Helped a teacher to set up guided reading groups and organized materials for instruction.
* Prepared and distributed Literacy Place lesson planners for teachers.
* Worked with teachers to review *Wiggleworks,* a computer program for beginning readers.

As the list suggests, collaborative resource management involves some tasks that are seemingly mundane (completing a book order) and others that will have an obvious broad impact down the road (helping teachers to organize books in the book room).

It is in this format of the continuum that coaches often raise the issue of how to draw the line between facilitating reflective resource management and simply becoming another pair of hands in reaction to a list of management issues that a teacher has to deal with. Let me share a personal example to highlight what I mean.

As a new coach in 1980, I was anxious to establish trust and garner respect. This was going quite well with many of the teachers I worked with. One teacher, however, decided that it would be most beneficial if I could run errands that she would otherwise not have time to do. In my effort to please, I allowed myself to become her preferred courier service rather than the trusted colleague I aspired to be! Sometimes, in order to build trust, we find we need to extend ourselves beyond the "typical" reach of coach. Generally speaking, though, literacy coaches must clarify our roles and responsibilities for teachers so that we don't spread ourselves too thin doing tasks that veer from the purpose of the professional learning.

What will elevate the mundane to more influential is the care that we take in broadening the task's effect on professional learning. As I work with a teacher to complete a nonfiction book order, for example, we can engage in conversation about the best match between the students and the books available, highlight attributes of effective nonfiction texts (graphs, big ideas, pictures, etc.), and encourage the teacher to consider student interests as she makes her choices.

🗁 Professional Learning

For literacy coaches looking for additional suggestions on how to assist teachers with resource management, I recommend the book *The Literacy Coach's Handbook: A Guide to Research-Based Practice* (2004) by Sharon Walpole and Michael C. McKenna. The authors include several chapters relevant to this topic.

Questions for Discussion

1. If you are a literacy coach, share some examples of how you have used resource management to build relationships with the teachers whom you work with. If you are not a literacy coach, share examples from your perspective.

2. Share some thoughts on how a literacy coach can walk the fine line between doing something for a teacher (to be helpful and build rapport) and standing aside to build capacity in the teacher.

3. Recall an experience when a colleague helped you to review curriculum materials or organize a literacy routine in your classroom. Was it a positive experience? If not, why not? If so, what did the colleague do that made it a positive experience?

4. When we are accomplished at something, we naturally want to show someone else how it *should* be done. As a coach, our job isn't to tell teachers how or what to do

(a short-term solution), but rather to help them reflect on their own practice. How might a literacy coach rein in the urge to engage in quick fixes that don't reap lasting consequences?

5. It's important that a coach's time be focused on the identified coaching goals and objectives. How does this principle apply to resource management?

4

Literacy Content Presentations

Literacy content presentations, the second format on the Literacy Coaching Continuum, provide the opportunity for a coach to share information with a group of teachers and ensure a common understanding of content, procedures, and best practice. I liken these presentations to minilessons—short, structured lessons on a topic relevant to the coaching focus goals and objectives, which themselves reflect student needs.

In research about professional learning, a number of studies show that subject-specific pedagogical content is related to the success of such efforts (Borko & Putnam, 1996; Cohen & Hill, 2000; Desimone, Porter, Garet, Yoon, & Birman, 2002; Little, 1993). Literacy content presentations provide opportunities to focus on subject-specific pedagogy. Good professional learning recognizes that teaching is an intellectual pursuit that requires engagement in content.

Content presentations can be opportunities to do the following:

- Introduce new information.
- Showcase the "big picture" by highlighting connections to other initiatives.
- Build and activate a learner's background knowledge.
- Clarify topics previously discussed.
- Pique the interest of teachers.

• Bring to the surface concerns about the implementation of a practice and allow for open discussion to voice trepidations, share successes and challenges, and encourage participants to collaborate on solutions.

• Identify issues for in-depth study, demonstration, and practice on the topic.

The Coach's Role

A literacy coach may have a variety of responsibilities in the area of literacy content presentations, including the following:

• Helping to train school staff in proper test administration procedures.

• Designing, planning, and conducting relevant training sessions at conferences, seminars, and workshops for small and large groups.

• Providing resources and training to school staff on scientifically based research and evidence-based practices in reading.

• Providing content knowledge and resources about teaching literacy skills.

• Providing information and guidance regarding a range of effective and innovative literacy practices through staff meetings and professional development or inservice training programs and workshops.

When planning content presentations, I keep in mind some advice from Thomas Guskey, a professor of educational policy studies and evaluation at the University of Kentucky. Guskey (1990) notes that teachers tend to learn about instructional improvements incrementally. For example, this year the teachers might be learning about cooperative learning; next year, the professional development focus might switch to text comprehension strategies, and so on. Although we assume that teachers are independently making the connections and will therefore integrate the information or infuse the practices into their daily routines, this isn't necessarily the case.

A role of school leaders, including literacy coaches, is to help teachers see the underlying connections among innovative practices and how these new practices fit in with what teachers are already doing. Of course, to make the connections between innovative practices explicit, those connections must first be real. Guskey (1990) suggests five guidelines for integrating innovative strategies into an improvement program:

• All strategies in the program should share common goals and premises.

• Remember that no single innovative strategy can do everything or solve every problem.

• The innovative strategies in the improvement program should complement each other.
• All innovative strategies must be adapted to individual classroom and building conditions.
• When a well-conceived combination of innovative strategies is used, the results will likely be greater than those attained using any single strategy. (pp. 13–14)

Guskey's article is a good one to share at a professional learning meeting for coaches. It is available on the ASCD Web site.

Planning the Presentation

With Guskey's general recommendations in mind, let's look at some specific suggestions for planning a literacy content presentation.

In my work with schools, I recommend using a planning form to guide the content presentation process. Figure 4.1 shows an example. A template for this worksheet is available for download on the ASCD Web site, but coaches should feel free to modify their planning form to meet local needs. I suggest keeping a copy of the filled-in form as a record of the event and as a source of information for later reflection.

I've also found that it's advisable to form a collaborative planning team to establish the content focus and the agenda for the session. If we are recommending that teachers learn to collaborate, it is helpful to model the practice.

A content presentation should always begin with a quick review of the pertinent data that form the basis for the minilesson. For example, if fluency is the content focus, it makes sense to draw attention to school and classroom data that provide the rationale. Although some people may like receiving a stack of handouts about effective literacy practice, not everyone feels the same. Handouts should be brief and to the point. Less is more when it comes to information that we want people to use. Attaching a copy of the handouts to the filled-in planning form provides a record of the material that has been disseminated. Reading Rockets (see Figure 4.2) is a good source for handouts.

PowerPoint slides can be helpful in moderation. Personally, I struggle to maintain interest when a presenter scrolls through a seemingly endless series of slides while reading the content verbatim. Using a few slides to highlight key points in the presentation or to pique interest is a better use of this medium.

If the presentation includes information about "how to do" a specific instructional technique (for example, repeated oral reading to increase reading fluency), it's a good idea to demonstrate the procedure. Video or audio vignettes of students, such as those

DOWNLOAD

Figure 4.1   Worksheet for Planning
a Literacy Content Presentation—Completed Sample

Date of Session: 09/26/07   **Location:** Library

Planning Team Members: Joe, Mary, Jose, Donna

Audience: Elementary teache rs and assistants   **Number of Participants Expected:** 15

Literacy Goal:
Teachers will know how to choose vocabulary words for instruction.

Content Objective(s):
Teachers will
• Understand what it means to "know a word"
• Be able to define "Tier Two" words
• Know the criteria for recognizing Tier Two words
• Be able to identify Tier Two words

Measures of Success:
Using a text that their students will be reading, participants will generate a list of all words that are likely to be unfamiliar to their students. They will then analyze the word list to determine the Tier Two words that they will need to teach for comprehension.

Inclusion of Tier Two words in instructional plans.

Potential Links to Participants' Current Practice:
Highlight specific children's books in their classroom libraries that are particularly helpful for teaching vocabulary words.

Next Steps:
☑ Decide on and gather data to be presented.
☑ Prepare handout(s). Attach a copy for the record. Done (9/20/07)
☑ Prepare PowerPoint slide(s) to highlight key points. (Jose will compile the presentation)
☐ Choose video vignette(s), if available.

Other:
1. Change the lesson plan form we currently use to include a list of Tier Two words to be included in the instruction.
2. Review strategies for introducing vocabulary.
3. Provide participants with a copy of *Bringing Words to Life* by Isabel L. Beck, Margaret G. McKeown, and Linda Kucan.

Figure 4.2   Resources for Literacy Content Presentations

Handouts
Reading Rockets is a national multimedia project offering information and resources on how young children learn to read, why so many struggle, and how caring adults can help. Go to http://readingrockets.org/ and click on "Articles from A–Z."

Video Vignettes
Annenberg Media provides professional development programming for K–12 teachers. Go to http://www.learner.org/. Among the available videos are the following:

- *Teaching Reading K–2: A Library of Classroom Practices*
- *Teaching Reading K–2 Workshop*
- *Engaging with Literature: A Video Library, Grades 3–5*
- *Engaging with Literature: A Workshop for Teachers, Grades 3–5*
- *Teaching Reading: 3–5 Workshop*
- *Making Meaning in Literature: A Video Library, Grades 6–8*
- *Teaching Multicultural Literature: A Workshop for the Middle Grades*

---

recommended in Figure 4.2, can supplement the demonstration. In addition, if the expectation is that the participants will try the instructional routine before the next session, the presentation should include some time for practice.

Here are a few more ideas for making the most of literacy content presentations:

- Make a connection to other innovations or "chunks" of information that teachers have been using to link the new information to prior knowledge.
- Showcase curriculum resources associated with the presentation topic.
- Discuss next steps.
- End the session with a tangible task that teachers can try in their classrooms.

Literacy content presentations are best as bite-sized servings of information. After the subject matter is shared, teachers will need time to ruminate on the conversation and consider how it blends with their current practice. It's important for literacy coaches not to offer more than can be digested in one sitting. It took me a long time to appreciate the concept of quality versus quantity.

From 1980 to 1998 I was the Special Education Training and Resource Center Trainer at the Otsego Northern Catskill Board of Educational Cooperative Services in

Stamford, New York. This is a statewide network of professionals that helps local districts develop, implement, and evaluate plans based on best practice to improve student achievement. Many of my assignments involved working with classroom teachers of newly mainstreamed students with disabilities. Early in my tenure, I also operated under the mistaken impression that more information was always better, and I jam-packed my workshop agendas with more than I could possibly do justice to—and more than teachers could comfortably sit through. As if the overflow at content presentations were not enough, I would also give participants stacks of handouts to take home. Did I really think that teachers would engage in self-tutorials when they got back to their classrooms?

Today I take time to review my professional learning plans with colleagues to ensure that I'm not going overboard in terms of the amount of content I think I can cover. I choose my handouts carefully using the following questions to guide my choices:

• Do the handouts I have chosen highlight the big ideas covered in the content presentation?

• Are the connections between the presentation and the handouts clear?

• Are my handouts repetitive? If so, choose the best one and omit the rest.

• Are my materials presentable? Are they clear and formatted to provide easy access to the information?

• Is there a way that I can use the handout during the presentation to illustrate the usefulness of the information (e.g., provide some true/false statements and ask participants to refer to handouts to find the response)?

Questions for Discussion

1. Think of a content presentation that you recently attended. What attributes of the session made it a positive learning experience?

2. I compare a content presentation to a minilesson. Given what you know about mini-lessons, what are your thoughts about my analogy?

3. The content presentation should focus on the coaching goals and objectives. What are some examples of this alignment?

4. Guskey suggests that helping teachers see the connections between innovations will help them to integrate new practice into their classroom routines. What are some ways this idea can be incorporated in content presentations?

5. What is the connection between data analysis and content presentations?

5

Focused Classroom Visits

Focused classroom visits, the third format on the Literacy Coaching Continuum, are opportunities for teachers to observe their colleagues at work and thus extend their own professional learning. Unlike the kind of classroom observation most familiar to educators, the purpose of focused classroom visits is not to evaluate the teacher under observation but to illuminate the teacher doing the observing.

The key word here is *focused*. The classroom visit, which is facilitated by the literacy coach, must have a specific purpose—one that is aligned with the goals and objectives of the coaching program. Examples might be watching a specific literacy routine (such as a writer's workshop), observing how another teacher organizes for instruction (such as the use of flexible grouping procedures), or checking out how another teacher instructs students on using a particular text-comprehension strategy. If a teacher is learning how to implement a new reading program, it helps to observe a colleague who is experienced with the program use the material in a classroom setting. If two teachers observe in the same classroom, they can share perspectives on their observation with each other.

Focused classroom visits allow teachers to do the following:

- Gain familiarity with new literacy practices.
- Observe a new spin on a known practice.
- Activate their prior knowledge.

- Generate questions about implementation of a new practice.
- Establish collaborative partnerships with fellow teachers.
- Learn about literacy instruction expectations at other grade levels (for example, a 1st grade teacher visits a 2nd grade classroom and vice versa).
- See how other teachers organize for literacy instruction.
- Watch how others use support materials (software, for example) in literacy instruction.
- Acquire a focus for conversations about a real classroom experience.
- Reflect on their own instructional processes.
- Develop insights to share with others.
- Get positive reinforcement about some of their current techniques.
- Realize a commonality of purpose in the role of teacher.

The Coach's Role

The coach's role in focused classroom visits is to serve as a facilitator. These are the primary responsibilities:

- Be on the lookout for teachers who can demonstrate best practice.
- Help teachers arrange for structured visits.
- Help visiting teachers identify key questions to guide their observations.
- Encourage visiting teachers to take notes that capture their reactions to the key questions.
- Facilitate the debriefing conversation with the teachers who observed and help them plan how to integrate new insights and information into practice.

The literacy coach helps to identify a classroom that the observing teacher can visit to see a specific practice in action in response to that teacher's desire to learn about or gain confidence in implementing it personally. It's the literacy coach's responsibility to match visiting teachers with the right demonstrating teacher. For example, a teacher who is interested in learning more about instruction in text comprehension needs to visit the classroom of a teacher who can provide a good model of text-comprehension instruction and is comfortable with the materials, familiar and adept at the routines involved, and able to differentiate the procedures based on the needs of real students—in other words, someone with at least "expert and adaptive knowledge," as articulated by Snow and colleagues (2005). The goal is for the visitors to see best practice in action; this can be done within the same school or by going to another location.

Some districts make the matching easier by compiling a directory of teachers who are willing to open their doors for focused classroom visits. The list includes their names, contact information, and what they are willing to share as their area of expertise. For the coach, conveying the importance of the reflective nature of classroom visits and the need for a focus are two of the most important features of this coaching format.

🗁 Professional Learning

Teachers and literacy coaches should prepare for focused classroom visits by practicing the skills and protocols of an observation. The following professional learning modules in Part III can help support this effort: **Module 12: Preparing for a Focused Classroom Visit** and **Module 13: Carousel Brainstorming on Focused Classroom Visits.**

The Process

Before the visit, the literacy coach has a brief discussion with the observing teachers to highlight the visit's focus, identify some key things to look for, and discuss ways for the teacher to record observations. At this time, the teacher may wish fill out a planning form, like the example in Figure 5.1. The visiting teacher and the coach can then use observational notes in a debriefing conversation. These reflective conversations are an essential feature of the process and lead naturally to discussions about follow-up. Figure 5.2 provides some guidance on the post-visit exchange.

I want to stress again that focused classroom visits are not evaluative in nature. They are *not* an opportunity to critique the lesson, classroom environment, teaching methods, or materials used by the teacher being observed. *The intent is for the visiting teacher to gather information to support self-reflection.* It is the visitor's role to listen, to observe, to record questions related to the focus of inquiry, and to respect classroom rules and procedures. For some, this assignment can be difficult. Self-reflection does not come easily to everyone. It is a muscle that needs to be exercised to grow stronger, and initially we are apt to fall back on our old patterns of response.

One of these old patterns is the tendency to judge the work of others: *their* lesson, *their* classroom, *their* methods. Comments such as "She should have prepared more

---

Figure 5.1   Worksheet for Planning a
Focused Classroom Visit—Completed Sample

DOWNLOAD

Name: Tina

Inquiry Focus:
To observe a literature circle in action.

Demonstrating Teacher and Classroom:
Mrs. Field's 6th grade classroom.

Pre-Visit Preparation:
I will make contact with demonstrating teacher to

☑ Confirm the agreed-upon observation time: Tuesday, February 12, 10 AM.
☑ Share questions (via e-mail by Feb. 9)
☑ Review inquiry focus and classroom rules and procedures. (via e-mail)

Other: Find out the titles of the books students are reading prior to my visit.

What I Hope to Learn:
The logistics of literature circles: how often, how many students, choosing books, etc.

Questions I Have for the Demonstrating Teacher:
• What are your suggestions for a teacher who is just introducing literature circles to a group of students for the first time?
• How do you choose the "right" book for a group of students? Do you choose it, or do the students?

Next Steps:
Introduce literature circles to my students.

---

questions for that activity" or "His room was too cluttered" divert attention from self-reflection. When we focus on someone else, we distance ourselves from involvement and put the onus of responsibility on the other person. If we are rating someone else's performance, classroom set-up, materials, or students, we are not thinking of how *we* will manage *our* lesson, or the best way *we* can use the materials, or how best to group *our* students. Going down this path of evaluative commentary diminishes our collective capability. It pits teacher against teacher and sets a subtle but destructive precedent for future conversations. It is the literacy coach's responsibility to frontload information to teachers that makes clear the purpose of the focused classroom visit. It is also the coach's duty to revisit the purpose before the debriefing conversation, and to redirect the conversation as needed during the debriefing session itself.

Focused classroom visits fit within the larger goals of stronger school leadership, high-quality professional development, and improved classroom instruction. Blase and Blase (1998) found that successful leaders support and promote collegiality by encouraging teachers to visit one another's classrooms to observe. Linda Darling-Hammond (1998) notes that high-quality professional development tends to include tasks that are "experimental, engaging teachers in concrete tasks of teaching, assessment, observation, and reflection" (p. 5). Darling-Hammond and McLaughlin (1995) also assert that teachers need multiple and ongoing opportunities to learn how to question, analyze, and change instruction to teach challenging content to diverse students. Focused classroom visits provide these opportunities.

Figure 5.2   Reflecting on a Focused Classroom Visit

A literacy coach can adapt these prompts to the needs of the observing teacher, remembering that the important thing is that a reflective conversation takes place that revisits the observing teacher's stated inquiry focus.

1. Share with me your focus of inquiry for the classroom visit.

2. What were you hoping to learn?

3. Were there any surprises?

4. Is this a lesson/procedure that you would like to replicate in your classroom? If so, are there adaptations/modifications you might make for your students?

5. What evidence did you see that the students were engaged in learning?

6. As a result of your observation, what additional questions do you have?

7. What are your next steps?

8. What supports would be helpful to you at this time?

An Example from the Field

An example of the systemic use of focused classroom visits as part of a district's professional development plan is the "intervisitation and peer network program" in Community District 2 in New York City, which was initiated by then-superintendent Anthony Alvarado. Administration and staff in District 2 recognized that "isolation is the enemy of instructional change" (Elmore, 1997, p. 8) and institutionalized teacher-to-teacher visits to observe exemplary practice by committing more than 300 days of professional time to this activity. Their investment in knowledge-sharing strategies (Fullan, 2001) was systematic and focused. Intervisitations in District 2 are one part of a reform effort (along with peer networks and instructional consulting) that aligns with seven organizing principles of instructional change outlined by Elmore and Burney (1997):

- The effort focuses on instruction and only instruction.
- It recognizes that instructional improvement is a long, multistage process involving awareness, planning, implementation, and reflection.
- It acknowledges shared expertise as the driver of instructional change.
- It focuses on systemwide improvement.
- It is built on the principle that good ideas come from talented people working together.
- It focuses on setting clear expectations, then decentralizing implementation.
- It recognizes that collegiality, caring, and respect are paramount if the effort is to succeed.

In 1998, Anthony Alvarado left District 2 to become the chancellor of instruction in the San Diego City Schools, where he continued his style of innovation and respectful leadership. For detailed information about the innovations spearheaded by Alvarado and his team, read Michael Fullan's book *Leading in a Culture of Change* (2001).

Getting Past "the Twinge"

Despite my many years of teaching experience, I still feel a twinge when a colleague asks to observe my classroom or workshop session. The part of me that appreciates collegiality is delighted to participate in the process of focused classroom visits, but lurking in the recesses of my brain are small doubts: What if an activity doesn't go as planned? What if one student (or workshop participant) isn't engaged in the agenda? What if the way I do things strikes the person visiting as mistaken or wrong? What if . . . what if . . . what if?

The good news is that my twinge now recedes very quickly. My confidence is partly due to years of experience, but mostly it's the result of many positive collegial interactions—the accumulation of upbeat experiences designed, facilitated, or celebrated by organizations, colleagues, and administrators who knew that good teachers can become better teachers when they are supported in their practice. A literacy coach might not be able to establish this kind of positive, collaborative atmosphere right away, but can certainly help create it over time through careful oversight of the focused classroom visit format.

☐ Professional Learning

The October 2006 issue of the National Staff Development Council's newsletter *T3: Teachers Teaching Teachers* features an article titled "Dear Colleague, Please Come for a Visit" (Lock, 2006). It's worth tracking down for additional ideas on how to implement focused classroom visits. Contact the National Staff Development Council at 800-727-7288 for information on how to access the issue or to subscribe to the newsletter in the future.

Questions for Discussion

1. Share an experience in which you observed in another teacher's classroom. What made the visit helpful?

2. What do you think should be included in a list of guidelines for etiquette during classroom visits?

3. How can a literacy coach support focused classroom visits?

4. What are some ways literacy coaches might ensure that the teachers they work with understand how critical self-reflection is to the focused classroom visit format?

5. Imagine you are a literacy coach working with a visiting teacher who, despite your initial prep work, responds to the visit by critiquing the classroom or the teacher. What might you do during the debriefing session to steer the conversation toward a more productive path? What might you do the next time around to ensure that the focused classroom visits remain self-reflective in nature?

6

Coplanning

The fourth learning format on the Literacy Coaching Continuum is coplanning. During coplanning, the literacy coach and the teachers work together to analyze current data and plan subsequent instruction with these data in mind. The data should focus on the coaching goals and objectives that have been articulated. For example, if vocabulary instruction is a focal point, teachers might discuss information garnered from a specific assessment tool, view demographic information about a child's language learning experiences, and share insights from differentiated instructional plans.

Reflecting on what demographic, outcome, and process data (see Chapter 1, p. 8) will round out the discussions will help the coach and teachers determine which additional information and resources to have on hand. This planning process might include discussions on grouping options, alignment to learning standards, potential teaching tools, and ways to infuse content knowledge into lessons.

The Coach's Role

Coplanning involves the following responsibilities for the literacy coach:

• Coplan lessons and curriculum units with teachers based on a systematic study of student needs.

• Work with teachers to align instruction to learning standards.

• Set goals and plan lessons with teachers based on analysis of student assessment data.

• Examine students' ongoing performance data to identify needs, monitor progress, and modify instruction for struggling readers.

What the Literature Says

There is a great deal of literature about coplanning and coteaching available to inform the literacy coach's practice (Bauwens, Hourcade, & Friend, 1989; Cook & Friend, 1995; Reinhiller, 1996; Sevakis & Harris, 1992; Vaughn, Elbaum, Schumm, & Hughes, 1998). Much of it focuses on inclusion and the collaboration between regular and special educators, but the guidance offered in these materials is universally applicable.

Friend and Cook (1996) define interpersonal collaboration as "a style of direct interaction between at least two co-equal parties voluntarily engaged in shared decision making as they work toward a common goal" (p. 5). They highlight some defining characteristics of collaborative relationships. Such a relationship is voluntary, is based on parity, requires a shared goal, and includes shared responsibility and accountability. Increased positive experience with collaboration results in the growth of trust and mutual respect.

Judith Warren Little (1982) found that more effective schools could be differentiated from less effective schools by the degree of teacher collegiality found within them. She articulated four categories of behaviors that were attributes of collaboration:

• Teachers communicated regularly and talked explicitly about instruction.

• Teachers observed one another in the classroom and served as critical friends.

• Teachers coplanned together, designing, evaluating, choosing, and using instructional materials.

• Through their collaboration, teachers taught one another about the practice of teaching.

Little uses the term *joint work* to highlight opportunities for coplanning, such as researching materials and ideas for curriculum, preparing lesson plans, making collective agreements to test an idea, and analyzing practices and their effects. Staging a collaborative planning agenda around a lesson design template will enhance coach-and-teacher conversations by keeping this joint work on track and student focused. In *The Art and Science of Teaching*, Robert J. Marzano (2007) recommends that a lesson plan design have three main attributes: (1) segments likely to be part of every lesson, such as an anticipatory set, objectives and purpose, modeling, and opportunities for guided and independent practice; (2) segments that focus on academic content; and (3) segments that address immediate necessary action, such as information about how to engage students in the work and the use of cooperative learning.

Marzano also offers a set of action steps that can help a literacy coach and class-room teachers articulate a lesson design outline. Interwoven with these is a series of questions that can guide a collaborative team's decisions on how to structure a lesson for best results and accountability and guide its post-lesson reflection. I also recommend his "Questions for Daily Reflection" (p. 190) as excellent prompts for facilitating coplanning conversations.

Examples from the Field

A well-known model of coplanning is lesson study, which I mentioned in Chapter 2. Catherine Lewis (2002), a senior research scientist at Mills College in Oakland, California, describes lesson study as an opportunity for teachers to do the following:

• Formulate goals for student learning and long-term development.
• Collaboratively plan a "research lesson" to bring those goals to life.
• Conduct the lesson, with one team member teaching and others gathering evidence on student learning and development.
• Discuss the evidence gathered during the lesson, using it to improve the lesson, the unit, and instruction more generally.
• Teach the revised lesson in another classroom, if desired, and study and improve it again.

Lewis, Perry, and Hurd (2004) point out that lesson study "is not just about improving a single lesson. It's about building pathways for ongoing improvement of instruction" (p. 18). Creating one "perfect" lesson is a discrete skill. Learning the attributes of student-focused lessons to improve achievement is building connective tissue. Chokski and Fernandez (2004) articulate this notion by stating that "the central idea of lesson study is that it is meant to be a generative process through which teachers continually improve and redirect their teaching as needs arise from their students and classrooms. Lesson study is therefore not meant to be a vehicle for teachers to assume an entire set of static teaching practices. On the contrary, it is intended to encourage teachers to adopt practices based on dynamic experiences and deep reflection" (p. 524).

Teachers who engage in this form of collective coplanning increase their knowledge of content and pedagogy. They become more astute observers of children and are therefore more likely to design lessons that will challenge and motivate their students. The process brings coherence to instruction by linking the day-to-day practice of teaching to long-term goals and objectives. Participation in lesson study can strengthen a teacher's sense of efficacy: the belief that improvement in teaching is not only possible, but a lifelong component of being an effective educator.

Fernandez, Cannon, and Chokski (2003) identified three challenges that American educators face when using lesson study model. First, they tend to be uncomfortable applying a research lens to their teaching, which means framing their work in inquiry, generating a hypothesis, collecting evidence, and generalizing their findings. American educators also have difficulty looking at lesson study through a comprehensive curriculum lens, preferring instead to adopt an order of instruction developed by textbook publishers without critically appraising the validity of these decisions. Finally, they have trouble using a student lens to review and evaluate their instructional planning.

Recommended Resources for Coplanning

Under the direction of Catherine Lewis, the School of Education at Mills College in Oakland, California, hosts a Web site highlighting resources and research on the topic of lesson study. You can access the information at www.lessonresearch.net/index.html.

The National College for School Leadership (n.d.) in the United Kingdom has developed an excellent series of booklets designed to teach participants how to use lesson study to "help slow lessons down." Booklet 1, *Network Leadership in Action: Getting Started with Networked Research Lesson Study,* introduces readers to the process and explains the rationale for usage, provides a "Quick Start" guide, and suggests a step-by-step approach for implementation. Booklet 2, *Networked Research: Lesson Study in Practice,* offers snapshots of practice including usage in core subject areas, pedagogical approaches, and cross-curricular settings. Booklet 3, *Networked Research Lesson Study: Tools and Templates,* offers sample tools to support implementation of the process. Included are approaches to data collection, lesson plan templates, and forms for collecting information about measuring professional development outcomes. Clearly written and smartly designed, these booklets are an excellent resource to share with teachers who are interested in trying the lesson study model. All three booklets are available from the organization's Web site. You can access them by visiting www.ncsl. org.uk/ and following the "Publications" link.

The United Kingdom also provides a notable example of coplanning in action. Teachers at Dulwich Hamlet Junior School in England participate in joint lesson planning and review using a "Learning Conversation" protocol. This planned, systematic approach to professional dialogue supports teachers as they reflect on their practice. As a result, teachers gain new knowledge and use it to improve their instruction. On a weekly basis, teams of teachers (three in each team) meet to plan the following week's work. Teachers report that these planning sessions have been the most helpful form of professional development:

> One teacher gives as an example: "You say to one of the others 'have you tried that activity? It was a nightmare' and if they say 'it worked really well for me' then you have to ask yourself what it was about the way you did the activity that made it go less well. You really reflect on your teaching." The teachers talk about the power of accessing the experience of three people rather than just one before making a decision, and the range of areas they discuss—the curriculum, organizational approaches such as ability grouping, children's different learning styles. Other teachers talk about the motivation which comes from these conversations. "Somebody will be excited by something and that rubs off on the rest of us." (General Teaching Council for England, n.d., para 3)

Literacy coaches can play a critical role in the initiation, facilitation, and continuance of lesson study and other forms of coplanning by collecting information about the process, facilitating discussion of its potential, helping to clarify teachers' roles, and supporting action research that sustains the collection and analysis of data related to the process of lesson study. (See Chapter 2's related discussion of the literacy coach's role as school research coordinator.)

Lessons from Experience

During my career I have had many opportunities to work with teachers in a coplanning capacity. I have also had colleagues with whom I could collaborate to enrich and refine my professional practice. In my current position as senior literacy specialist, my primary work is in the area of professional development. Coplanning is an essential feature of my job. Everything I do involves cooperative planning to some degree.

In 1999, I met my colleague Elizabeth Powers, a senior project associate at the Mid-Atlantic Comprehensive Center at George Washington University in Washington, D.C. Since that time we have cooperatively planned and implemented hundreds of professional development sessions as part of our systemic work with school districts. We have coplanning down to a science, and not only is the process beneficial to the work that we do, but it's a lot of fun as well.

We tend to start our cooperative efforts by generating a quick list of essentials that we intend to cover in the workshop session. This list is based on a concise review of data, which in our case might include reviewing feedback forms from earlier sessions, revisiting the coaching goals and objectives, and identifying a focus for the upcoming session. One of us takes notes that we then turn into a follow-up "facilitator outline" so that we can designate who will work on which section of the agenda.

We usually collect our potential resources (research, articles, activities) before our next conversation and then use the collaboration time (via phone) to do a dry run of our respective planned components. This process allows us to be critical friends to each other as we hammer out the final plan. The aspect of coplanning that brings the process full circle is our debriefing conversation after the program is over.

As a result of our work together, I have generated the following tips for coaches:

• Work only with teachers who indicate an interest in coplanning. You can't make someone collaborate—nor should you want to.

• Model coplanning by asking teachers to engage in cooperative planning around coaching policy, content, and format issues.

• Establish and maintain trust by following through on your promises.

• Build rapport by getting to know your coplanning partner or partners.

• Identify and capitalize on personal and professional strengths that each person brings to the partnership.

• Focus on the coaching/teaching goal.

• Develop a planning protocol that *you* are comfortable with. Use this template to frame your collaboration and keep you on track.

• Celebrate and learn from your successes.

• Recognize when things don't go as planned, and learn from the challenges.

• Use data to guide your planning. Make sure that modifications and adaptations are grounded in sound research and practice.

• Remember that coplanning is about reciprocity, not grandstanding.

When the collaborative relationship is working well, it seems natural and can result in a renewed rigor and relevance to the work produced. When the relationship isn't working well, it's painful, and the outcome seems like more trouble than it's worth. I expect that many readers have experienced this—the sense that "it would be easier to do this on my own!" Coplanning relies on the relationships between the people who are working together. Success can't be forced, but it can be nurtured.

Questions for Discussion

1. Think about your own experiences with coplanning. Can you identify what you consider to be important elements of the process?

2. What "rules of etiquette" would you recommend for coplanning?

3. In your school, what opportunities exist to learn from others through lesson planning and review?

4. What information do you think should be on a planning form to guide the process?

5. What is the literacy coach's role in facilitating coplanning meetings?

7

Study Groups

The fifth learning format on the Literacy Coaching Continuum is study groups, a commitment by a group of educators to meet regularly to focus on an instructional issue. As a professional learning format, study groups have been around for a long time. Many years ago, when I first started teaching in Vermont, I was involved in an "issue discussion group." Of course, we didn't call it that then; it was our "midweek survival group," because as new teachers, we were desperate for a supportive setting where we could share ideas and resources. Every other Wednesday we would meet to talk about our students, our teaching, our concerns, and our celebrations. Perhaps because we were all novices, we didn't feel nervous about sharing our ups and downs. Our group had a number of benefits, not the least of which was reducing our sense of anxiety and isolation in the early days of our teaching careers.

Study groups can increase teamwork, provide occasions to share and solidify knowledge, support curriculum reform, offer opportunities for feedback from trusted peers, and develop a climate of professionalism. The operative word here is *can*. Simply arranging for a study group (or for any other format on the continuum) does not ensure that professional learning will take place.

In his book *Evaluating Professional Development*, Thomas Guskey (2000) suggests that to be effective, study groups must be well organized, be focused, and allow sufficient time to accomplish the tasks. Another helpful piece of advice he offers is to establish ground rules that disallow comments that begin with "I think . . ." and encourage the group to use language such as "research indicates _____." From my perspective, the important thing is to distinguish between *what we think* and *what we know* or *what is known*. It is appropriate for professionals to draw conclusions from the data at hand, as long as we are committed to rigorous review of our hunches in light of the research available.

Brian Lord (1994) identifies a type of professional learning that he calls "critical colleagueship" (pp. 192–193). His list of the characteristics of critical colleagueship, paraphrased here, resonates with me as a good way to describe a productive study group experience:

• Members experience *productive disequilibrium*. Although they are not certain of what the group's outcome will be, they are interested in the topic, engaged in the process, and essentially optimistic.

• Within the group, there is *encouragement for fundamental intellectual virtues* and *willingness to be empathetic with one's colleagues*. Group members are curious, conscientious, and open to considering new, different, and even contradictory ideas and perspectives. They are aware of themselves and their colleagues as capable professionals.

• There is a *focus on improving the skills of negotiation and communication*. The study group's protocols stress a commitment to clear communication and collective decision making, and this is reinforced by skillful facilitation on the part of the literacy coach or one of the team members.

• Group members experience *increasing comfort with ambiguity*. The more they learn about and reflect on the topic and its associated challenges, the less inclined they are to seek a "cookbook" solution.

• Group members achieve collective *generativity*—the knowledge of how to go on. As the group spends more time together, members figure out what actions to take and what direction to go in.

I recommend a report by Richard Meyer (1996), presented at an Annual Meeting of the American Educational Research Association and titled "Teachers' Study Group: Forum for Collective Thought, Meaning Making and Action." It's a delightful narrative about the "passion and pain" of teacher inquiry, and it includes transcripts from study group sessions, logistical information about setting up your own study group, and insights gained from the process. As Meyers eloquently states, "Teacher groups . . .

are about discovering the possibilities for ourselves, within and among and between ourselves, and with the children with whom we live in schools. The groups are a forum, a thought collective, a safe harbor, and they support teachers as we create schools as places for thinking, growing, inquiry, and learning" (p. 119). You might also want to seek out Meyer's book on the same topic, *Composing a Teacher Study Group* (1998).

The Coach's Role

Literacy coaches play an important role in the initiation, implementation, and maintenance of study groups. The literacy coach's responsibilities in this area include the following:

• Provide study group participants with information and guidance regarding a range of effective and innovative literacy practices.

• Plan the focus of teacher study groups by analyzing assessment information in reading and writing for assigned classrooms and using the information to inform practice.

• Establish groups with shared leadership in mind. I advise literacy coaches not to hold on to the controls so firmly that your colleagues will feel uncomfortable taking over the facilitation.

• Locate resources for study groups. For example, write a grant to purchase professional books or collect articles of interest to be read by participants.

• Model the study group process to showcase the protocol members should use to structure the meetings.

• Lead a discussion of group norms.

Types of Study Groups

In the publication *Teacher Study Groups: Building Community Through Dialogue and Reflection*, Birchak and colleagues (1998, p. 19) provide a "menu" of various kinds of study groups, which I have summarized in the list that follows. To amplify their category descriptions, I've added some examples.

1. *School-Based Groups.* These are composed of educators within a particular school. (Teachers at the same school meet each week in the literacy coach's room to discuss an agreed-upon topic.)

2. *Issues Discussion Groups.* These are groups formed to address questions and concerns about a shared issue. (Teachers at the same school get together to review lesson plans and to share relevant resources.)

3. *Readers and Writers Groups.* These are formed to discuss literary works or pieces of writing. (A small group of teachers meets to read poetry to enhance their own appreciation of the genre and to inform their instructional practice.)

4. *Professional-Book Discussion Groups.* These groups are initiated by a common interest to read a professional book or set of articles. (Teachers read and discuss *Mosaic of Thought* by Keene and Zimmerman. Between sessions, they try out some of the text comprehension strategies in their classrooms.)

5. *Teacher Research Groups.* These groups are composed of educators who come together to discuss their systematic, intentional classroom inquiries. (Staff meet to review assessment results to determine next steps for instruction.)

6. *Topic-Centered Groups.* These are composed of educators from different schools who are interested in the same topic or issue. (All 4th grade teachers in the district focus on fluency instruction. They share articles on specific instructional procedures, practice using the techniques, and discuss how to demonstrate the procedure to their students. They implement the practice in their classrooms before the next meeting and then discuss the outcomes.)

7. *Job-Alike Groups.* This kind of group is composed of educators who have the same type of position in different schools. (Members of a committee on special education meet to discuss recent changes in the Individuals with Disabilities Education Act and implications for their literacy instruction. One participant shares information about Response to Intervention, and the rest of the group discusses the implications for literacy intervention models.)

Not all study groups start out with an in-depth discussion of student data, but it is advisable to link the establishment of a group to information about student needs. The link between professional learning and student achievement should be transparent, and the only way to achieve this is to establish a deliberate connection between the two early in the professional learning initiative. (This is true of all formats, by the way, not just study groups.) For example, in order to determine a focus of study on the topic of fluency, group members would need to answer questions such as these: *Why are we studying fluency? What do we know about our own students' fluency? What does research tell us that can help our students to become more fluent readers? How is fluency* related to comprehension? What role does vocabulary play in fluency? What do we currently do to address the fluency needs of our students? How will the study group (or content presentation or demonstration lesson) help us to better serve our students?*

Establishing a Study Group with Data at the Core

Although each study group "type" has characteristics that distinguish it from the others, there are some general guidelines for establishing and maintaining a study group that can be helpful.

First, it's important to remember that a study group is more than just a gathering of individuals talking about a particular topic; it is a serious form of professional learning *focused on an instructional issue*. In most cases, data, such as formative or summative assessment results, can help with the initial determination of what issue or issues the study group should focus on. Data should continue to inform the discussions throughout the study group's duration. The following is a step-by-step guide that the literacy coach can use to establish and maintain a study group with data as the driving force:

1. Ask this question: *What do we need to study that will result in better instruction for the children we work with?* An example response might be that children are struggling with comprehension because they don't have the content-specific vocabulary needed for understanding. Therefore, we need to emphasize vocabulary acquisition in content classrooms and determine the best ways to do this.

2. Assemble the group, limiting its size to no more than six members.

3. Determine what kind of data would be most helpful in answering the question in Step 1. Examples might be survey data on the vocabulary that students need to know in each content area; teacher feedback on how they currently teach content-specific vocabulary, whether it's working, and for whom it's working (for some students? for all students?); and specific data about student acquisition of content-specific vocabulary.

4. Gather the data.

5. Analyze the data.

6. Answer this question: *Does the group need any additional information at this point?*

7. Answer this question: *What specific things do we need to study or learn about that will result in better instruction for our students?* Example responses might be that the group needs to learn to assess students' knowledge of content vocabulary, needs to learn methods to teach key vocabulary words, and needs to learn new ways to provide

extra vocabulary instruction for students who need it. The emergent study group focus might read like this:

> We will discuss assessment procedures we can use to measure success.
> – We will study and discuss methods we can use to teach key vocabulary words.
> – We will implement one of the strategies we learn about with our students and use this group as a sounding board to reflect on the outcomes.
> – We will discuss intervention methods for students who might need additional support.

8. Determine how the group will measure the professional learning's impact on student achievement. An evaluation protocol, such as the ones developed by Guskey and Killion, can guide this process. The key question to answer is this: *What evidence will we accept to show we have accomplished what we set out to do?*

9. Decide on the study group format (job-alike, book study, and so on).

10. Establish and keep a regular schedule, letting no more than two weeks pass between meetings.

11. Practice distributed leadership, in which group members take turns acting as meeting facilitator.

12. Establish group norms at the first meeting of the study group. Post these group norms on the wall at each meeting.

13. Develop an action plan that might include one or more of the following:

- Conduct research.
- Examine student work.
- Seek resources.
- Read and study material.
- Contact coaches or speakers.
- Design lesson plans and activities related to the coaching focus.
- Try out lesson plans and activities related to the coaching focus.

14. After each meeting, complete a Study Group Log, clarifying members' responsibilities, action steps, and measures of success. The group might opt to share this log with the rest of the faculty on a regular basis.

15. Monitor the plan by continuing to review the data on a regular basis.

16. Revisit the purpose of the study group. Study groups do not need to last a long time to be effective. If the group members have completed the work they set out to do,

it might be time to disband and move on to another format in the Literacy Coaching Continuum (or another study group).

What the Research Shows

Research supports the value of study groups as an effective form of learning for teachers. The U.S. Department of Education sponsored a three-year longitudinal study of approximately 300 teachers and found that the most effective professional development was typically characterized as a "reform type" (e.g., teacher networks or study groups) that involved *the participation of teachers from the same subject, grade, or school* rather than the traditional workshop or conference (Porter, Garet, Desimone, Yoon, & Birman, 2000).

In 2003, Dr. Russell Gersten was awarded a Teacher Quality grant from the U.S. Department of Education to conduct a study to evaluate the effectiveness of teacher study groups as part of professional development for 1st grade reading teachers. A Web site for the Teacher Study Groups Project (www.lehigh.edu/collegeofeducation/cprp/projects/tsgp_website/tsgp_open.htm) has been established to disseminate the results as they become available.

As noted in Chapter 2, in Saginaw, Michigan, 95 percent of teachers have participated in a study group focused on implementing literacy strategies to enhance student achievement. In "The Saginaw Teacher Study Group Movement," Weaver, Rentsch, and Calliari (2004) credit their project with the systemic implementation of a new reading initiative and subsequent improvements in their student achievement data. They further note that the model has been successful in

- Strengthening schoolwide reading goals through peer feedback.
- Identifying strong programs and best practices.
- Disseminating innovations and models among staff.
- Expanding the reading initiative's impact.
- Assessing the school's progress toward stated reading goals and objectives.
- Demonstrating accountability for meeting reading goals.
- Capturing the authentic study and resulting work of a project. (pp. 38–39)

This account will be a helpful resource to literacy coaches who are interested in pursuing study groups because it offers advice and guidance on all aspects of the process, from inception through evaluation.

Maryellen Brunelle (2005) studied the impact of job-embedded, collaborative study group meetings on the creation of a professional learning community and teachers' literacy instructional practices. From October to April, seven primary teachers and their researcher/principal met bimonthly to examine and discuss the literacy work of their low-achieving students. Subsequent data analysis indicated that the study groups led to the development of a shared vision of practice and purpose. This is no small thing, considering how important it is to have common ground when implementing best practice. It also showed evidence of other attributes of a professional learning community, including more consistent and reflective sharing of instructional techniques and assessments. Ultimately, the study groups led to better integration of guided reading and a greater emphasis on writing.

Study groups provide an ideal venue for engaging in critical colleagueship. I encourage literacy coaches to explore the resource materials in Part III's Module 6, which support efforts to organize, facilitate, and maintain momentum in study groups.

Recommended Resources for Study Groups

My personal preference when it comes to choosing "just right" books for study groups is to avoid inspirational texts—books that deal with big ideas but don't articulate a specific plan of action—and gravitate instead toward books that review the research base of a specific topic and provide practical suggestions for implementation and assessment. The goal is to choose a text that can not only inspire deep conversation about research-based best practices but also provide clear and relevant scaffolds for these practices' implementation and refinement.

A good example is Timothy Rasinski's book *The Fluent Reader: Oral Reading Strategies for Building Word Recognition, Fluency, and Comprehension* (2003). Readers of this book learn the importance of fluency to a child's growth in reading, see the links between fluency and other aspects of literacy development, get new ideas about how to assess fluency, and gain a toolkit of instructional procedures that can help a child become a more fluent reader. Teachers who read this book can practice the assessment and instructional procedures between the study group's meetings. They can collect student data before, during, and after integration of the instructional procedures into classroom practice.

Figure 7.1 lists books I recommend for study groups. I also encourage literacy coaches and their groups to seek out their own "just right" books that are suited to specific group aims within their school.

Figure 7.1   Resources for Study Groups

Phonemic Awareness
Phonemic Awareness in Young Children by Marilyn Jager Adams, Barbara Foorman, Ingvar Lundberg, and Terri Beeler (1998)
Phonemic Awareness Activities for Early Reading Success by Wiley Blevins (1997)

Phonics
Words Their Way: Word Study for Phonics, Vocabulary, and Spelling Instruction by Donald R. Bear, Marcia Invernizzi, Shane R. Templeton, and Francine Johnston (2000)
Phonics They Use: Words for Reading and Writing by Patricia M. Cunningham (1999)

Vocabulary
Bringing Words to Life: Robust Vocabulary Instruction by Isabel L., Beck, Margaret G. McKeown, and Linda Kucan (2002)
The Vocabulary Book: Learning and Instruction by Michael F. Graves (2005)
Word Power: What Every Educator Needs to Know About Teaching Vocabulary by Steven A. Stahl and Barbara Kapinus (2001)

Text Comprehension
Comprehension Instruction: Research-Based Best Practices edited by Cathy Collins Block and Michael Pressley (2002)
Mosaic of Thought: Teaching Comprehension in a Reader's Workshop by Ellin Oliver Keene and Susan Zimmermann (1997)
Reading for Understanding: A Guide to Improving Reading in Middle and High School Classrooms by Ruth Schoenbach, Cynthia Greenleaf, Christine Cziko, and Lori Hurwitz (1999)

Fluency
Reading Pathways: Simple Exercises to Improve Reading Fluency by Dolores G. Hiskes (2007)
The Fluent Reader: Oral Reading Strategies for Building Word Recognition, Fluency, and Comprehension by Timothy V. Rasinski (2003)
Fluency Instruction: Research-Based Best Practices edited by Timothy Rasinski, Camille Blachowicz, and Kristin Lems (2006)

Adolescent Literacy
When Kids Can't Read: What Teachers Can Do by Kylene Beers (2002)
Building Academic Literacy: Lessons From Reading Apprenticeship Classrooms Grades 6–12 edited by Audrey Fielding, Ruth Schoenbach, and Marean Jordan (2003)

Writing
Wondrous Words: Writers and Writing in the Elementary School by Katie Wood Ray (1999)
When English Language Learners Write: Connecting Research to Practice K–8 by Katherine Davies Samway (2006)

Literacy Assessment
Assessment for Reading Instruction by Michael C. McKenna and Steven A. Stahl (2003)

Miscellaneous
Using Data to Assess Your Reading Program by Emily Calhoun (2004)

📁 **Professional Learning**

See the following modules in Part III for suggested activities and materials related to study groups: **Module 4: A Guiding Protocol for Data Analysis; Module 5: Paired Reading on Data Analysis;** and **Module 6: Jigsaw of Study Group Formats.**

Questions for Discussion

1. Based on your personal experience, what advice would you give to teachers who are interested in participating in a study group?

2. What are some professional texts that you think would be appropriate for book study groups?

3. I refer to some helpful advice from Thomas Guskey (2000) regarding study groups. He recommends establishing ground rules that disallow the "I think" comments and encourage the group to use language such as "research indicates." What do you think about this suggestion?

4. What information do you think ought to be in a Study Group Log?

5. What do you see as the literacy coach's role in the study group process?

8

Demonstration Lessons

The sixth learning format on the Literacy Coaching Continuum is demonstration lessons. Demonstration lessons offer teachers the opportunity to see a literacy coach deliver a lesson and to reflect on how they might apply what they see to their own practice.

There are three main purposes for demonstration lessons:

• To demonstrate particular teaching methods, strategies, or content to teachers who are less familiar or confident with them.

• To provide a common experience of teaching that can serve as the basis for discussing and developing practice.

• To foster teachers' self-reflection and creative problem solving.

As part of the literacy coaching continuum, demonstration lessons yield the most benefits when they are closely aligned with established coaching objectives.

All professionals, teachers included, tend to feel more confident about taking on something new after they have observed someone else putting the new practices in action. It's not a surprise, then, that demonstration lessons are a common form of learning outside of the traditional classroom.

For example, I like project-oriented vacations, and a few years ago, I decided to spend my vacation in the Adirondacks taking a class on rustic furniture making. The program flyer advertised that at the end of the week, participants would leave the workshop with a footstool and a chair. That alone was enough to convince me that this was the vacation I was looking for!

The session began with an overview by the instructor. He asked us questions about our prior woodworking and building experience (mine was almost nil), shared information about the history of rustic furnishing, showed slides of past and present examples, and reviewed the highlights of the coming week. In other words, he built our readiness for the task at hand. For the rest of the week, he followed a pattern of explicit modeling and "gradual release of responsibility" in action (although I doubt that he would have called it that). My classmates and I had many demonstration lessons; the one focused on making a mortise and tenon joint—a simple way of joining two pieces of wood in a 90-degree angle—followed this sequence:

1. *Pre-assessment: Identify student needs.* The instructor queried my classmates and me to find out what we knew—and didn't know—about building furniture.

2. *Modeling: I do/you watch.* The instructor made a mortise and tenon, and I watched.

3. *Sharing expertise: I do/you help.* The instructor made a mortise and tenon, and I helped.

4. *Gradual release: You do together/I help.* My classmates and I made a mortise and tenon, and the instructor helped us as needed.

5. *Assessing mastery: You do/I watch.* I made a mortise and tenon. The instructor watched.

Wilhelm (2004) refers to this progression as the "sequential process of teaching" (pp. 36–37).

Obviously, completing one course on making rustic furniture hasn't made me an expert, but I do feel pleased whenever I look at my chair and footstool (and their mortise and tenon joints). Surely a gradual accrual of satisfaction, combined with supportive scaffolds, would eventually lead to expertise—in building furniture or in building a teacher's confidence and capacity. Therefore, it is helpful to think of demonstration lessons or instructional modeling as the "I do/you watch" component of the Literacy Coaching Continuum.

The Coach's Role

The role of the literacy coach in the area of demonstration lessons includes the following responsibilities:

• Demonstrate research-based best practices in instruction for teachers at a wide range of experience levels, or arrange for others to teach the lesson. In the case of demonstrations, the person teaching the lesson should have at least a stable, procedural grasp (see Figure 1.1, p. 12) of the content or strategy.
• Conduct planning sessions with teachers before the demonstration lesson.
• Conduct debriefing sessions with teachers after the demonstration lesson.

Aspects of a Demonstration Lesson

In her book *Pathways: Charting a Course for Professional Learning,* Marjorie Larner (2004) suggests that demonstrations can vary in their level of teacher participation. As she puts it, "Once I have established a working relationship with teachers, I begin coteaching with them rather than demonstrating while they just watch. At first, I may lead the teaching and welcome teacher contributions to the discussion. Then the teacher and I may model a discussion of our thinking about a text. As the relationship grows, it becomes natural to play off each other in the teaching time, asking questions, challenging opinions, and providing feedback" (p. 50).

This quote illuminates an important fact about demonstration lessons: mutual decisions made by the literacy coach and the teacher will determine the nuance of the coach's demonstrations. A coach must always keep in mind this format's overarching purpose: to share a common experience of teaching that can be a springboard to reflective conversation focused on the coaching goals.

Larner (2004) also suggests that demonstration lessons can vary in their level of teacher participation. From this perspective, demonstration lessons are a natural fit with coteaching, the last format on the Literacy Coaching Continuum (see Chapter 10). Larner defines demonstration lessons and coteaching as "a tightly focused, purposefully planned session that provides an opportunity for teachers to see a particular instructional strategy, usually in the context of their own classroom or school" (2004, p. 47). The terms "tightly focused" and "purposefully planned" are key components of her description.

To ensure that a demonstration lesson has a clear focus and a purposeful plan, it is important to follow an organized structure that consists of (1) a brief meeting during which the coach and the teacher prepare for the demonstration lesson, (2) the demonstration lesson itself, and (3) a debriefing session.

The Preparation Meeting

At the preparation meeting, the teacher and the coach should discuss the context of the lesson and the key features of focus. This is the time for the coach to give a very quick overview of the lesson to be demonstrated. For example, if the purpose of a lesson is to introduce story structure analysis using a graphic organizer, such as a story map, the coach and observer might look over the chart, preview the children's book to be used, and discuss potential questions the students might have about the process.

To ensure adequate preparation for a demonstration lesson and clarify the lesson's design for the teacher, I recommend that the literacy coach and the observing teacher complete a planning template, like the example shown in Figure 8.1. This form (available for download on ASCD's Web site) prompts the teacher and the coach to articulate the lesson's learning goals for students, making explicit reference to standards and data-based student needs and the lesson's coaching goals. It also helps break the lesson into clear steps, which helps the teacher and the coach focus on literacy strategy integration and set some specific focus questions for the observing teacher.

The Demonstration Lesson

During the demonstration lesson itself, the observing teacher should generally do just that: observe what the coach is doing and resist the temptation to join in. In some cases, it may be appropriate to talk to some of the students when the class is working informally in groups. It is important to work out in advance who—the coach or the observing teacher—will address any behavior management issues that arise. (Planning for this possibility should be part of the preparation meeting.) The observer may also find it helpful to make a few brief notes on the specific focus of the demonstration lesson to refer to during the debriefing session. For both the coach and the observer, it is important to remember that lessons do not always go as planned. The coach who is teaching the lesson may have to deal appropriately with an unpredicted response from the class, rather than stick rigidly to the plan. These sidetracks from the plan often lead to the best conversations and provide an opportunity for the coach to reinforce the concept that change is a given in the teaching arena!

Figure 8.1   Worksheet for Planning a
Demonstration Lesson—Completed Sample

DOWNLOAD

Learning Standards Addressed:
New York State Language Arts Standard 2: Speaking and Writing
Key Idea: Listening and reading for literary response involves comprehending, interpreting, and critiquing imaginative texts in every medium, drawing on personal experiences and knowledge to understand the text, and recognizing the social, historical, and cultural features of the text.

Focus Area:
Performance Indicator – Elementary: "Use inference and deduction to understand the text."

Supporting Data:
Analysis of the Primary Reading Comprehension Strategies Rubric (available at the Mosaic of Thought Toolkit Web site: www.u46teachers.org/mosaic/tools/tools.htm – Strategy Rubrics K–5) shows that the majority of Mrs. Smith's students are at a level one for inferring and do not "make predictions, interpretations, or draw conclusions."

Coaching Goal(s):
1. Demonstrate a "think aloud" and the connection of the tool to strategy instruction.
2. Share resource with the observing teacher that will be helpful to students learning how to make inferences (Kendall & Khuon's *Making Sense: Small-Group Comprehension Lessons for English Language Learners*).
3. Review the special challenges ELLs face when learning to make inferences:
   — Idioms and figurative language in text
   — Unfamiliar vocabulary
   — Homonyms and synonyms
   — Difficult text structure (topic sentence, supporting details, and conclusion)
   — Connotative and denotative meaning of words
   — Confusing story themes and endings
   — Imagery and symbolism

Description of the Lesson to be Demonstrated:
1. Review meaning of "inferring" with students using the Mosaic of Thought Toolkit poster available at www.u46teachers.org/mosaic/tools/tools.htm.
2. Read aloud the book *Tight Times* by Barbara Shook Hazen. Talk about the cover to provide time for thinking and listening. Point to specific parts of text to provide comprehensible input to English language learners.
3. While reading, model a think-aloud. Show thinking using sticky notes. While modeling making predictions, ask students to agree or disagree using a "thumbs up/thumbs down" signal.
4. Ask students: "Who can describe what I just said and did as I read the book?"
5. Give students sticky notes to record their thinking during the remainder of the read-aloud.
6. When the story's complete, ask students to share inferences with a partner.
7. Lead a group discussion: "What did we learn by making inferences during the story, and how else could we use this strategy?"

Focus Questions for the Observing Teacher:
1. What did I do during the demonstration lesson that was helpful to ELL students?
2. Why is a "think aloud" a helpful tool to use when teaching about literacy strategies?

The Debriefing Session

The debriefing session, or postobservation analysis and discussion, is just as important as the preparation. It should

- Take place soon after the lesson.
- Be scheduled at a time when the teacher and the coach will not be interrupted.
- Provide an opportunity for the teacher and the coach to walk through the main parts of the lesson.
- Focus on the specific aspects the observer wanted to see.
- Encourage and support teachers in reflecting on their own practice in light of the demonstration lesson that they observed.
- Provide an authentic transition to "next steps" for teacher action.

The coach should use the debriefing session to encourage self-reflection and creative problem solving by the teacher, *not* to tell the teacher what to do or not to do! If certain issues regularly arise during debriefing sessions with teachers, the coach should keep a list of such issues to inform future professional development. It's important that professional learning be cohesive and make sense within the context of a real classroom. By following the threads of conversation that proceed from the demonstration lesson, you can spin them into meaningful patterns or identify missing links for subsequent discussions.

🗁 Professional Learning

For more on demonstration lessons, please see **Module 8: The Demonstration Lesson: Planning Meeting; Module 9: The Demonstration Lesson: Debriefing Session;** and **Module 10: The Demonstration Lesson: Discussing the Debriefing Session.**

Some coaching programs deliver demonstration lessons by establishing lab classrooms where teachers can go to observe a specific practice. The Arkansas Comprehensive Literacy Model advocates this use of model classrooms. In other programs, the coach visits a colleague's classroom to model demonstration lessons. This is the case in the Boston Plan for Excellence's Collaborative Coaching and Learning Model, where each cohort of teachers observes a demonstration lesson focused on their area of inquiry. The demonstration lesson always takes place in the classroom of one of the participating teachers.

One of the things that I really appreciate about demonstration lessons is that they take adult professional learning into the classroom. Schools are places where we all should and could be learning. I have always found that students are pleased to see that their teachers are learners too, and they quickly become comfortable with the notion that their lessons are part of an adult learning lab.

Recommended Resources for Demonstration Lessons

There are a number of resources I can recommend for readers interested in learning more about demonstration lessons. One is *An Introductory Guide for Reading First Coaches*, from the Vaughn Gross Center for Reading and Language Arts at the University of Texas at Austin (Central Regional Reading First Technical Assistance Center, 2005). This publication shares some prompts that can be used during the debrief conversation, such as "How did the coach use scaffolding? How did the coach integrate students' prior knowledge and skills?" It also provides some sample forms, such as a Classroom Observation Form and a Reflection/Post-conference Planning Sheet, which can be used as coaching protocols.

In *Cognitive Coaching: A Foundation for Renaissance Schools* (Costa & Garmston, 2002), the authors provide a transcript of a reflecting conversation (a debriefing session). This transcript is helpful because it points out the facilitative role that the coach assumes to encourage teachers to self-reflect on their own students and instructional practices. Reviewing this information may help coaches to generate their own prompts for use in future debriefing sessions. Lyons and Pinnell (2001) offer some creative ways for coaches to demonstrate teaching approaches, including live demonstrations, videotape, simulation, and distance learning.

Questions for Discussion

1. Share some examples of demonstration lessons that you have been involved in, either as a demonstrator or as an observer. What went well? What would you do differently the next time? What advice would you share with colleagues?

2. What do you see as the literacy coach's role in facilitating demonstration lessons?

3. I advise that the observer should focus on observing, not joining in. Do you agree with this advice? Why or why not?

4. Videotaped lessons are a creative way to conduct demonstration lessons. What do you see as the challenges of this method, and how might you counteract them?

5. What are your thoughts about the establishment of model classrooms (as in the Arkansas Comprehensive Literacy Model)? What do you see as the advantages of this approach?

9

Peer Coaching

Peer coaching, the seventh learning format on the Literacy Coaching Continuum, is the activity most traditionally associated with coaching. In the peer coaching format, it is the *coach* who observes and offers guidance and ideas based on the current practices of the teacher under observation.

Some peer coaching models assume there will be a formal literacy coach assigned to guide each teacher; other models assume that classroom teachers will take turns coaching one another. Slater and Simmons (2001) see peer coaching as the latter and share a definition first proposed by Pam Robbins (1991): "a confidential process through which two or more professional colleagues work together to reflect on current practices; expand, refine, and build new skills; share ideas; teach one another; conduct classroom research; or solve problems in the workplace" (1991, p. 1).

Neither model is better; it's a matter of deciding which approach best fits the needs of your school and teachers within the context of an overall literacy coaching program. For example, if a teacher has indicated an interest in learning how to administer a specific assessment instrument, it would make sense for a trained literacy coach, who knows how to implement that procedure with fidelity, to be the one to demonstrate it. Then, two teachers who have observed the demonstration might go on to serve as peer coaches for colleagues.

Peer coaching is often a good format to use following demonstration lessons. Teachers have had the opportunity to see the coach model a lesson, and they want (or the coach encourages them) to give it a try. At the risk of sounding like a broken record, I will stress that the focus and content of the lesson should proceed from data on student needs.

The Coach's Role

The literacy coach's responsibilities with the peer coaching format are as follows:

- Share the purpose and process of peer coaching: to allow teachers to discuss the impact of their instruction, to problem solve, and to reflect on their practice while working to improve student learning.
- Suggest that teachers who are going to serve as peer coaches observe a demonstration lesson together.
- Explain that if the literacy coach observes, the same process applies. Make it clear that the observation is not evaluative.
- Facilitate conversations with colleagues about the issue of feedback. Share the differing perspectives of coaching models. For example, in an Expert Coaching Model, the coach explicitly demonstrates or teaches and then observes the teacher to check for understanding and confirm by practice. In other peer coaching models, feedback is purposefully omitted, as the emphasis is on the reflective conversation that occurs.
- Reinforce and act on the notion that it is the teacher who is in the driver's seat. The teacher defines the parameters of the observation and lays the groundwork for the debrief conversation.

A Three-Step Process

The peer observation cycle typically involves three steps: the pre-observation meeting, or planning conference; the actual observation; and a postobservation debriefing session (Barkley, 2005; Costa & Garmston, 2002; Gottesman, 2000; Robbins, 1991).

The Pre-observation Meeting

The pre-observation meeting is an opportunity for the teacher to "paint a picture" of the lesson to be observed for the person who will be observing, either a formal literacy coach or a peer coach. This conversation includes discussion of the lesson's focus, procedures the teacher will follow, materials the teacher will use, any information about the students that is pertinent to the lesson, and other details about the classroom environment that might be helpful to the observer. For a lesson focused on using oral language prompts, for example, the teacher might use the pre-observation meeting to say this to the literacy coach: "In my math class, I'm going to try out some of the oral language prompts that you shared with us—the ones that are helpful to English language learners (ELLs). I've written out some of the prompts on chart paper that I can choose from. I think this will be helpful to all my students but particularly so for the ELLs. Would you keep track of the prompts I use so that we can talk later about the responses and reactions these triggered in the students?"

Some teachers are initially uncomfortable in this "lead" role and are hesitant to talk about their lesson or verbalize the action they want the coach to engage in during and after the observation. I think this is because professional learning in education is often very prescriptive and doesn't leave a lot of room to fully explore the act and art of teaching. In my experience, when teachers are regularly asked to identify their learning needs based on student data, they come to do so with confidence.

The focus of the observation is determined by the goals and objectives that have been identified as part of the planning process for the coaching. For example, if the goal is to have students use strategies to construct meaning from print, the teacher might ask the coach to observe a minilesson on inferring, and to keep track of the prompts that the teacher uses to support students' use of the strategy.

The planning conversation also provides an opportunity for the coach to ask clarifying questions about the lesson to firm up the focus of the observation. Such questions might include the following:

- Are there students I should pay particular attention to?
- Are there specific aspects of the lesson that you would like me to focus on?
- Would it help my observation if I looked over the materials to be used in the lesson? (Giving teachers this option may help them to organize for the lesson.)
- What information would you like me to collect during the observation? (When working with teachers who are not yet used to defining their own professional learning, the coach might need to provide suggestions at this point: "You have mentioned that you wonder how to pick up on clues that students are getting or not getting what you're trying to teach. Would it be helpful if I keep track of student comments after you give your directions? Maybe we can notice a pattern.")

The coach should conclude the planning conversation by repeating back the agreement for observation and data collection: "I'm really looking forward to seeing your math lesson. So, I will be keeping track of student comments that indicate that they understand or don't understand your directions. Is that correct?" At this time, too, the coach should confirm the arrangements for the visit: time, place, and where in the classroom the teacher would like the observer to sit.

The Observation

During the observation, the formal or peer coach records the "events" of the lesson as they unfold. These might include conversations or exchanges between the teacher and students and any matters pertinent to the stated focus. In other words, the observer records what is happening in the classroom but does not impose opinions or interpretations on the information. Given this objective stance, you can see why it's important to have a planning conversation before the observation. If the approach is to "wing it," coaches will tend to look at things that *they* think are important, as opposed to focusing on the center of attention that the teacher has identified.

The Debriefing Session

The postobservation debriefing session between coach and teacher ideally occurs on the same day as the observation. This meeting allows a reflective conversation about the lesson that took place.

The stance and strategies used during this conversation will depend on the model the coach has chosen to implement or the perspective that resonates for the coach and teacher involved. For example, Rita Bean (2004) suggests three ways that a coach can work with the teacher during the postobservation meeting: (1) coach as mirror, (2) coach as collaborator, or (3) coach as expert. In the first approach, the teacher is self-reflective and quickly assumes a leadership role in the conference; the coach confirms and validates what the teacher articulates. In the second approach, the coach and the teacher collaboratively analyze and reflect on the lesson, working together to determine its strengths and possible weaknesses. In some instances, such as with novice teachers or when something new is being tried out, the third approach allows the coach to serve as an expert who can help teachers effectively implement various strategies or approaches.

Others view the postobservation conference as an opportunity for teachers to flex their metacognitive muscles. In *Cognitive Coaching,* Arthur L. Costa and Robert J.

Garmston (2002) have a supportive perspective on what internal capacities an accomplished (my word) teacher brings to the table. They refer to "states of mind" (efficacy, flexibility, consciousness, interdependence, and craftsmanship) and view the role of the coach as a mediator who uses skills and strategies (such as rapport, meditative questioning, response behavior, pacing, and leading) to stimulate teachers' thinking about their practice. They consider the "reflecting conversation" the vehicle to attain this goal.

Bruce Joyce and Beverly Showers (2002) write that in the 1980s, they believed that feedback was an important component of the coaching cycle. In their current practice, however, they omit feedback as a coaching component because they have found that technical feedback is laden with distracting implications; teachers view it as "first the good news, then the bad." They also found that coaches tend to drift into supervisory roles, which is counter to what they feel coaching is all about. According to Joyce and Showers, "the primary activity of peer coaching study teams is the collaborative planning and development of curriculum and instruction in pursuit of their shared goals" (p. 88), and they argue that their research indicates this new spin on the coaching process has not "depressed implementation or student growth" (p. 89).

Variations on the Three-Step Process

Bean (2004) delineates an additional step in her articulation of the model: planning, observing, *analyzing/reflecting,* and conferring. She specifies the need for the coach to take time to analyze and reflect on the observation in preparation for the post-observation conference with the teacher. In this phase of the coaching cycle, the coach reviews the notes or script recorded during the observation to determine the best strategy to use to engage the teacher in reflection about the lesson. Bean offers some key questions that the coach might consider in this reflection:

- What are the key points to raise?
- How do I want to start the conference?
- What changes would best improve the instruction going on in that classroom? Are the changes doable? What support would the teacher need for implementing the changes?
- What approach might be best in working with this teacher?

The Instructional Coaching Model at the Kansas University Center for Research on Learning also adds a twist to the mix by conducting a precoaching interview—a one-on-one conversation between the teacher and the coach to gather information, establish rapport, and explain the program framework. You can read more about this helpful process in Jim Knight's book, *Instructional Coaching: A Partnership Approach to Improving Instruction* (2007).

As you can see, the peer coaching theme has a number of variations. I recommend the coach and teacher consult with peers, consider the options, and choose the approach that feels most comfortable. Coaches who are fortunate enough to be involved in a learning network with other coaches can use that network as a vehicle for reviewing their thoughts with a colleague. Obviously it is important to respect the confidentiality of the teacher who has been observed, so no names or other identifying information should be shared.

Becoming an Accomplished Teacher

Teaching is an intellectually challenging vocation. An accomplished teacher has to consider the diverse needs of a large group of students and help students "negotiate" the curriculum (Boomer, 1992). The accomplished teacher understands the implications of assessment and instruction and appreciates the importance of ongoing reflection. An accomplished teacher is a problem solver, understanding that if students aren't learning, solutions are rooted in action, not negative reaction. An accomplished teacher communicates, collaborates, and challenges perceptions. An accomplished teacher realizes that there are times when academic content must take a back seat to a caring conversation, and that children learn best when they are treated with kindness and respect.

Peer coaching is a professional learning tool that can provide opportunities for support and renewal for teachers so that they can become accomplished. It provides time for teachers to "see" themselves in action, and to engage in conversations about their practice. Often, this observed reflection of their teaching allows them to consider things they might have overlooked in the past and to make decisions that will affect their future practice.

As you evaluate the progress of your coaching program on a regular basis, you will review the impact of the peer coaching cycle. Teachers and coaches will find it helpful to debrief and discuss what they felt went well in the process, what they would do differently the next time, and what changes in practice they expect will result in increased student achievement.

Questions for Discussion

1. I describe what I believe to be the attributes of an accomplished teacher. What attributes would you add?

2. What do you think are the essential ingredients of an effective peer coaching conversation?

3. In what ways does peer coaching encourage reflective thinking?

4. What additional questions might be important to ask in the planning conversation?

5. What is your opinion regarding feedback to teachers after an observation? Do you agree with Joyce and Showers (see p. 87), or do you have another point of view?

10

Coteaching

Coteaching is the eighth and final learning format on the Literacy Coaching Continuum. In coteaching, two colleagues—a teacher and a literacy coach—work collaboratively to enrich the educational experience for all students in a classroom. By working together in this way, both the teacher and the coach can gain many ideas for implementing research-based practices in a structured and engaging environment.

A teacher and a coach might agree to coteach for a number of reasons, including the following:

• To engage in trial runs with planning, organization, delivery, and assessment of instruction.
• To collect data on delivery and assessment of instruction.
• To try things they wouldn't be willing to do alone.
• To develop knowledge and skills that might lead to greater student engagement or an increase in student achievement as a result of more focused instruction.
• To take advantage of diverse instructional styles and options.
• To develop skills for collaborating to enhance student achievement.
• To access another set of eyes to observe and help solve problems.
• To pair with another professional who has a different set of skills and talents.
• To engage in a shared opportunity for teaching that can be used as the basis for discussion.

Coteaching is not simply dividing classroom tasks and responsibilities between two people. It's also not the case of a coach stepping in to teach a lesson so that the teacher can step out of the classroom. It is, after all, a professional learning opportunity, and requires the involvement of both the teacher *and* the coach.

As noted in Chapter 6, there is a great deal of published information about coplanning and coteaching. Much of it is written from the perspective of a service delivery model in special education that seeks to increase educational access for students with disabilities. For example, here is how Cook and Friend (1995) define coteaching:

> Co-teaching is defined as two or more professionals delivering substantive instruction to a group of students with diverse learning needs. This approach increases instructional options, improves educational programs, reduces stigmatization for students, and provides support to the professionals involved. Co-teaching is an appropriate service delivery approach for students with disabilities who can benefit from general education curriculum if given appropriate supports. Teachers and related service professionals who are flexible and have good judgment are likely to be successful in this role. Co-teachers need preparation, administrative support, and opportunities to nurture their collaborative relationships. (p. 20)

The authors go on to say that "Co-teaching programs should be planned and implemented systemically. Deliberate and ongoing communication among everyone involved is essential" (p. 20).

In special education, the term "coteaching" is typically understood as a permanent teaching assignment for a regular and special education team. In the context of the Literacy Coaching Continuum, it refers to periodic collaborative teaching involving a literacy coach and classroom teacher occurring for the purpose of professional reflection on shared teaching. Despite these differences, most of the aspects of the special education definition still apply. Let's examine those elements through the lens of literacy coaching:

• Teachers and coaches who are flexible are more likely to be successful in this role.

• Coteaching partners need preparation, administrative support, and opportunities to nurture their collaborative relationships (collaborative school structures, including equal-status rules for coaches and teachers).

• Coteaching should be planned and implemented systematically.

• Deliberate and ongoing communication among the coteaching partners is essential.

- Commitment to all students' learning is vital.
- Strong content knowledge is a necessary ingredient.

Roberta Murata (2002) refers to coteaching as "team teaching." As a teacher involved in team teaching over a three-year period, she found that having a common philosophy, especially in regard to curriculum and instruction, was an essential ingredient in the shared arrangement. Additionally, valuing depth over breadth was critical, and both teacher and student differences were perceived as strengths—an asset to the development of a collaborative community.

Kenneth Tobin has written extensively on the topic of coteaching in the context of science education as a framework for mentoring new teachers. His definition of coteaching is "premised on the idea that by working together with one or more colleagues in all phases of teaching (planning, conducting lessons, debriefing, grading), teachers learn from others without having to stop and reflect on what they are doing at the moment and why" (Tobin & Wolff-Roth, 2005, p. 314). In this model, the teaching collaboration is followed by a second step called "cogenerative dialogue," conversations among stakeholder groups (including students) focused on specific incidents occurring in the classroom. The intent of the reflective conversation is to "articulate salient elements of what worked and what did not work for the purposes of designing strategies for improvement, starting with the next lesson"(Tobin & Wolff-Roth, 2005, p. 315).

Tobin's Coteaching and Cogenerative Dialogue model encourages a shared sense of responsibility for the positive outcome of a lesson plan. For a more comprehensive examination of coteaching and cogenerative dialogue, you may want to read *Teaching Together, Learning Together,* edited by Michael Wolff-Roth and Kenneth Tobin (2005).

The Coach's Role

The literacy coach's responsibilities in coteaching include the following:

- Facilitate the articulation of collaborative lesson goals (e.g., writing and science, word problem solving and math).
- Develop lesson-planning protocols that can be used to coplan lessons.
- Oversee the coplanning process.
- Identify, in partnership with the teacher, the hoped-for outcomes of the process. Make a note of these for later discussion.
- Implement the literacy component of the lesson.
- Revisit the hoped-for outcomes during the debrief conversation.

• Make the learning transparent and point out connections between the coach's and teacher's efforts and the actual outcomes. Identify possible modifications for "next time."

• Plan for "next time."

An Example from the Field

In their report on using literacy coaching to change science teachers' attitudes about teaching writing, Leslie J. Hays and Cindy Davis Harris (n.d.) provide one example of what coteaching might look like in the Literacy Coaching Continuum. In an action research project, they investigated the following question: "What would happen to science teacher attitudes and beliefs about writing if a literacy coach were assigned to teach sentence-writing skills with the science teacher?"

In the school setting that the authors studied, the science teachers used a team approach to teach to common content standards. One of the standards was that students would write four formal lab reports, each six to eight pages long, to be evaluated using a departmental rubric. As you might expect, this literacy task presented a challenge for a large number of the students *and* for the science teachers.

Hays and Harris document the experiences of two high school science teachers who worked with a literacy coach. The coteaching model in this study required the literacy coach and the content area teacher to work together in teaching a lesson or an academic skill focused on writing strategies in the science classroom. Coaches will find much of value in this article (available online at www2.sjsu.edu/elementaryed/ejlts/archives/school_practice/Lesliehays.htm), which provides a model of action research, looks at the process from the coaches', teachers', and students' points of view, and realistically brings to the reader's attention some of the challenges of coteaching. It also reminds us of the purpose of this format in a coaching context: to bring together professionals with different skill sets to maximize the potential for student learning.

The content area teachers who participated in the study reported that they would not have implemented writing strategies into their instructional routines had it not been for the coteaching arrangement. This is significant when you think of the number of students who no doubt struggle with the writing component of science class.

In regard to student response to the study, two themes emerged in the analysis. One is that students reported more self-awareness about their use of strategies to support writing. The other is that students tended to relax their writing "know-how" (Hays & Harris, n.d., p. 9) based on what they perceived teachers wanted. Science teachers were seemingly unaware of the writing students are trained to do in English, and this was reflected in their rather low expectations for writing in science class.

The literacy coach made 24 classroom visits during the course of the study, half in her role as coteacher. In her analysis of the outcome, she noted three emerging themes: (1) students spent a large amount of time in class being passive recipients of information; (2) her observation and field notes were full of questions for teachers about how they check for understanding or make students accountable; and (3) there was "a certain amount of frustration, especially toward the end of the study, as the disconnect between what teachers were looking for in student work, their classroom practice and how students were telling us they learned best became more evident" (Hays & Harris, n.d., p. 11).

On the last day of the study, one of the participating science teachers sent the literacy coach an e-mail, which read as follows:

> I developed a worksheet that incorporates sentence writing. Are you proud of me? I am also spending some time today trying to work on thesis sentence writing for the next Formal Lab Reports! And, I think that I have some of the team hooked into doing it as well!! Here's to sentence writing! (Hays & Harris, n.d., p. 14)

Had these teachers not defined their coaching focus (sentence writing instruction in the science content classroom), documented their process, and analyzed the results, they would never have been able to clearly determine the challenges yet to address or what successes to celebrate.

Learning the Dance

Coteaching involves a sharing of responsibility for planning and delivery of instruction. You start with a lesson design template (such as the Worksheet for Planning a Demonstration Lesson in Chapter 8) and add your notations to the document to differentiate coteaching roles as you walk through the instructional planning steps. Another important element of the process is the debriefing conversation, which allows the coach and the teacher to discuss the lesson that took place and to consider future adjustments to the instruction. The classroom becomes a learning lab, and the teaching becomes transparent, so that subsequent instruction is deliberate and assessed on an ongoing basis.

Learning to coteach is a lot like learning how to dance. Toes may be a bit tender until coaches and teachers learn each other's style, stamina level, strengths, and stress points. Coaches, not wanting to overstep their bounds in another's classroom, may take timid steps at first. Teachers may be resistant, longing to shut the classroom door and work solo. Professional learning is about taking chances, because we are extending ourselves into potentially unknown territory, replacing familiar practice with new routines. Until the new routines become part of our repertoire, some discomfort is likely. Despite all of the challenges that coteaching entails, I quote the words in a song by Lee Ann Womack to express my final sentiment on coteaching: "And when you get the choice to sit it out or dance, I hope you dance."

Questions for Discussion

1. Which aspects of Cook and Friend's (1995) coteaching definition pertaining to special education apply to the model used by literacy coaches?

2. Cook and Friend observe that "co-teaching partners need preparation, administrative support, and opportunities to nurture their collaborative relationships" (1995, p. 20). What might collaborative school structures for literacy coteaching look like?

3. What do you think should be included as "rules of etiquette" for coteaching partnerships?

4. Have you ever been involved in coteaching? If so, describe some of the challenges you faced. Describe some of the benefits you gained.

5. How might you take the essential elements of coteaching and integrate these features into practice?

PART III

PROFESSIONAL
LEARNING MODULES
for Literacy Coaching

• • •

Introduction to the
Professional Learning Modules

It's never too late to implement an effective literacy coaching program that delivers differentiated professional learning.

If your current program doesn't have a defined theory of action, you can discuss it with your colleagues, analyze the data, and put together a plan of action based on the theory you develop. If you didn't carefully articulate the role of coaches from the onset, you can do so now. If you don't currently collect data to determine your instructional and coaching focus, you can use a protocol to guide the discussions and come up with a plan. This chapter provides ideas and materials for professional learning to initiate or improve a literacy coaching program.

Professional support for literacy coaches must be a valued component of every program, as exemplified by their initial preparation and the ongoing support they receive. My definition of *valued* assumes that this support will take priority over "things that come up" in the busy daily routine. All literacy coaches should be expected to attend the professional learning sessions and to participate in all exploratory experiences that will build and hone their skills. To make this happen, the building administrator needs to understand and share this value.

Coaching is a challenging position; the more skillful and informed coaches become, the better able they will be to collaborate effectively with their teaching colleagues.

The professional support provided must offer information and experiences in several areas:

• *Content knowledge of literacy.* This is an understanding of how students learn to read and read to learn.

• *Content knowledge of pedagogy.* This corresponds to what Shulman (1987) calls the "special attributes a teacher possesses that help him or her guide a student to understand content in a manner that [is] personally meaningful" (p. 8).

• *Knowledge of the coaching process.* This encompasses the skills and strategies related to the implementation, maintenance, and monitoring of a coaching program.

Participants in professional learning rarely work on these components in isolation. For example, during their meetings, coaches might take part in a study group that gives them experience managing a component of the Literacy Coaching Continuum while increasing their knowledge of a content topic.

The professional learning modules in this section are suggestions for ways to engage coaches and others in conversations about the work that they do to improve student achievement in literacy. The modules cover various aspects of planning, implementing, and monitoring a differentiated literacy coaching program. Keep in mind that while the guidelines in these modules will be helpful, the Literacy Coaching Continuum and the learning modules are yours to differentiate according to local needs and perspectives.

The Procedure section of each module is directed to the facilitator of the learning session. It is important to read through the entire module and the related figures and resources. In many cases, the module includes all the materials that are necessary for the learning session. In other cases, the facilitator will need to get recommended materials from online sources or elsewhere. The worksheets and templates available at this book's page on the ASCD Web site are indicated with a "Download" icon. Please note that when reproducing copyrighted articles and Web content for distribution in professional learning sessions, facilitators must be mindful of copyright restrictions. Always review the permissions guidelines associated with a piece in advance and secure proper permission before proceeding. The U.S. Copyright Office's guidelines for fair use are available at www.copyright.gov/fls/fl102.html.

Module 1
Guiding Questions:
The Planning Stage of Coaching

Time: 1–2 hours, depending on chosen extension activities

Participants: Literacy coaches, administrators, and teachers

Purpose:

- To invite participants to engage in focused conversations when planning (or rethinking) their coaching program.
- To generate a list of questions that will guide the planning process.

Materials Needed:

- Sentence strips with sticky backs, or paper and tape
- Markers
- Chart paper
- Handout: *Mentoring and Coaching for Learning: Questions for Schools,* a chart developed by United Kingdom's National College for School Leadership (n.d.). The chart is available for download at www.ncsl.org.uk/media/2FC/0F/randd-coaching-dfes-questions.pdf.

Procedure:

1. Divide participants into teams.
2. Ask each team to develop 10 questions that they believe must be answered thoroughly at subsequent planning meetings. These questions might address any aspect of literacy coaching, from logistics (e.g., schedules, coach qualifications) to the planned content focus. Have teams write one question per sentence strip or piece of paper and paste questions on their designated wall space.
3. Ask all participants to go to each station as a team to review their colleagues' questions.
4. Ask the participants to come up with a way to categorize the questions. Some examples might include *theory of change, logistics, content, coaching continuum formats,* and *evaluation.*
5. With the whole group, come to consensus about categories that best represent the range of team-generated questions.
6. Place chart paper on the wall and write the final categories (one category per sheet) on the chart paper, and ask each team to post their questions under the appropriate category.
7. The next step is flexible:
   – If time is available, use the questions to develop a template for gathering information about literacy coaching in preparation for the next planning meeting.
   – If time is short, end the meeting by explaining that you will type up the questions and that the participants will use the resulting template for the next planning meeting.
   – Ask participants to review the *Mentoring and Coaching for Learning* chart and then revise their list of questions based on this new information.

Module 2
Reviewing and Comparing Coaching Models

Time: 1 hour (minimum)

Participants: Literacy coaches, administrators, and teachers

Purpose:

- To provide participants with the opportunity to review a range of coaching models in terms of specific criteria, such as theory of change, roles, focus, administrator's role, and evaluation.
- To initiate conversations about the specific needs of a school's students and professional learning community.
- To identify the attributes of effective coaching models that a school might want to replicate.

Materials Needed:

- Handout: Worksheet for Comparing Coaching Models (Figure M2)
- Handout: Prepared information packets on various coaching models

Procedure:

1. Prior to the activity, collect information about a variety of coaching models. Appendix B lists Web sites that will be useful in tracking down pertinent information. Package the collected materials in large manila envelopes and label them individually with the name of the coaching model (e.g., "Collaborative Coaching and Learning [CCL]").

2. Begin the activity by telling participants that it can be helpful to look at a variety of coaching models as a way to initiate conversations about the specific needs of their students and their professional learning community. Explain these models include various philosophies, focuses, roles, evaluation procedures, kinds of administrative support, and professional learning opportunities available for literacy coaches, and talk about how examining these models can help them identify attributes that could be a good fit for their own literacy coaching program.

3. Group the participants into teams, each sitting at a separate table, if possible. At each table, post a placard with the name of one of the coaching models.

4. Hand out the coaching packets to each team to match the placard on their table. (The team at Table 1 gets information about Collaborative Coaching and Learning, Table 2 about Content-Focused Coaching in Elementary Literacy, and so on.) Give the team members 20 minutes or so to read and discuss the material.

5. Have each team collaborate to fill in a Worksheet for Comparing Coaching Models (Figure M2), using information about the model they reviewed. Feel free to customize this worksheet template as desired, removing some of the categories to provide a more focused analysis or adding additional ones of your own.

6. Engage the participants in a general discussion about the models.

7. As a follow-up, provide copies of the worksheet compilations to the full group. At subsequent meetings, participants can reflect further on their own perspectives and identify attributes of programs they might like to introduce in their own practice.

Figure M2		Worksheet for Comparing Coaching Models	DOWNLOAD
Name of Coaching Model			
Philosophical Basis			
Evaluation Procedures			
Schedule of Coaching Services			
Administrative Support			
Professional Learning Opportunities			

Module 3
Exploring Coaching Standards of Practice

Time: 1–2 hours, depending on procedures

Participants: Literacy coaches, administrators, and teachers

Purpose:

Depending on the procedure or procedures selected, this activity can be designed to do the following:

- Clarify the roles and responsibilities of a literacy coach.
- Encourage literacy coaches to target specific professional learning goals aligned to student achievement.
- Facilitate discussions about literacy across content areas.

Materials Needed:

- Handout: *Standards for Middle and High School Literacy Coaches*. This publication of the International Reading Association (IRA) (2006b) is available for download at the IRA Web site: www.reading.org/resources/issues/reports/coaching.html.

Procedure:

1. Divide participants into small groups and pass out copies of *Standards for Middle and High School Literacy Coaches*.

2. Ask small groups to review the document and do one of the following activities:

  – Activity A: Explore the text as a catalyst for their own action research.

  – Activity B: Discuss and determine their own professional learning goals and objectives, and share these with other staff at a later meeting.

  – Activity C: Compile a collection of personal vignettes of coaching-in-action as part of a reflective writing activity.

  – Activity D: Use the document at a teacher meeting (such as a study group or staff meeting) as a focal point to illustrate the importance of literacy across content areas.

  – Activity E: Use the document as a springboard for curriculum mapping by extending the initial conversations about literacy across content areas.

  – Activity F: Develop coaching and content teams to extend range and depth of expertise.

  – Activity G: Examine each objective through the lens of a special population, such as special education students, English language learners, and migrant students.

3. Hold a follow-up discussion with additional staff members to determine what other skill sets and knowledge base would be important to develop.

Module 4
A Guiding Protocol for Data Analysis

Time: 1–2 hours, depending on amount of time spent practicing protocol use
Participants: Literacy coaches, administrators, and teachers

Purpose:

- To introduce literacy coaches to a data analysis protocol.
- To discuss the advantages of using a protocol to guide discussion.
- To give participants the opportunity to engage in data-driven dialogue so that they may analyze and interpret data that could inform educational practice.
- To give participating teachers the opportunity to apply research-based instructional practices as informed by an analysis of available data.
- To show participants how to use the data to make instructional decisions and to inform the need for and the content of professional development.

Materials Needed:

- Handout: *User-Friendly Guidelines for Making Sense of Data,* based on a data analysis protocol by Dennis Fox (see Figure M4)
- Handout: "Guiding Instruction Through Assessment." This article by Dennis Fox (2004) is available from the Web site of the Association of California School

Administrators: www.acsa.org. Follow the "Publications" link to the excerpts from *Leadership* magazine.

- Sample literacy data compiled before the session (e.g., results from a phonemic awareness assessment)
- Chart paper and markers
- Chart or presentation slide showing the basic tenets of data analysis:

Basic Tenets of Data Analysis

- Use a protocol to guide the discussion.
- Have a planned agenda so that the group remains focused.
- Keep the group small.
- Meet regularly.
- Make the data public.

Procedure:

1. Introduce the participants to some basic tenets of data analysis by showing them the Basic Tenets chart.
2. Explain that in this session they will learn how to use a data analysis protocol developed by Dennis Fox and adapted by literacy coaches from the Lorain School District in Ohio.
3. Share the following definition of *protocol*, taken from the Web site Looking at Student Work (http://www.lasw.org/protocols.html):

   - A protocol consists of agreed-upon *guidelines for a conversation,* and it is the existence of this structure—which everyone understands and has agreed to—that permits a certain kind of conversation to occur—often a kind of conversation which people are not in the habit of having.
   - Protocols are vehicles for *building the skills and culture necessary for collaborative work.* Thus, using protocols often allows groups to build trust by actually doing substantive work together.

   Explain that there are other data analysis protocols that can be used; the important thing is to have a guiding template that is used consistently to keep the group focused on the task at hand.

4. Ask participants if they know of other protocols. If they do, invite them to share information about the template they use.

5. Share the User-Friendly Guidelines for Making Sense of Data (Figure M4), and walk the participants through this protocol using the sample data.

6. Explain to the coaches that when they first introduce the protocol to teachers it will be much easier to demonstrate the process using sample data rather than the teacher's own student data. Teachers new to literacy coaching may be sensitive about sharing their own student data because they worry that it might reflect badly on their instructional skill. Using sample data and letting them see how the collegial, noncritical process works increases their interest in exploring their own student information with the group.

7. Ask coaches to discuss how they will introduce the data analysis protocol to their colleagues.

8. As an extension activity, share the resources with participants and ask that they explore one of the sites on their own. Invite them to report back to the group about the resource at a follow-up meeting.

Print Resources on Data Analysis

Using Data to Assess Your Reading Program by Elizabeth Calhoun (2004)

A Guide for Evaluating a Reading or Language Arts Program by Roger Farr and Beth Greene (1999)

Stepping Stones to Evaluating Your Own School Literacy Program by Jeri Levesque and Danielle Carnahan (2005)

"First Things First: Demystifying Data Analysis" by Mike Schmoker (2003)

Online Resources on Data Analysis

Informing Practices and Improving Results with Data-Driven Decisions. This online-only article by the Education Commission of the States (2000) is available at www.ecs.org/clearinghouse/24/02/2402.htm.

Analyzing and Using Data. This online toolkit from the Maryland Department of Education (n.d.) is available at www.mdk12.org/data/index.html.

Sample Data Analysis Protocol. This online publication from the School District of Philadelphia (n.d.) has lots of resources, including reports of action research carried

out by teachers. The URL is http://phila.schoolnet.com/outreach/philadelphia/
teachersstaff/protocols/.

Figure M4   User-Friendly Guidelines for Making Sense of Data

Before we come to any conclusions about our data or make any decisions based on these data, we
must ask the following questions:

1. What do we *know* as a result of examining this data?
  a. List facts.
  b. List quantifiable statements.
  c. List statements that cannot be debated or argued about.

2. What do we *think* as a result of examining this data?
  a. List what we think this tells us about what students know and can do.
  b. List what we think this data suggest that students are struggling with.
  c. List the kinds of instruction we think are going on.
  d. List hunches we have.

3. What *don't* we know as a result of examining this data?
  List information that we cannot know just by looking at the data and, therefore, should not consider in our decision.

4. What do we *want* to know as a result of examining this data?
  a. List questions that we have about student performance.
  b. List questions that we have about teachers' instruction.
  c. Note other information we may need to look at.

5. How does/will this data help us improve instruction?
  The point of looking at the data is to prepare and plan for the most effective instruction to meet
  student needs. List some ways we might do that.

Source: Guided questions developed by Dennis Fox of the Southern California Comprehensive Assistance Center. The clarifying information after
each question was added by coaches of the Region III Comprehensive Center and Lorain City School District 201 in Ohio.

Module 5
Paired Reading on Data Analysis

Time: 1 hour

Participants: Literacy coaches

Purpose:

- To provide the opportunity for coaches to discuss the role of data analysis in professional learning.
- To introduce coaches to expert opinion on the topic.

Materials Needed:

- Handout: "Role: Data Coach," an article by Joellen Killion and Cynthia Harrison (2005). Members of the National Staff Development Council (NSDC) may download the article free of charge from www.nsdc.org. Nonmembers may purchase the issue by calling NSDC at 800-727-7288.
- Handout: "Using Student Outcome Data to Help Guide Professional Development and Teacher Support: Issues for Reading First and K–12 Reading Plans," an article by Joseph Torgesen, Jane Granger Meadows, and Patricia Howard (n.d.). It is available from the Florida Center for Reading Research at www.fcrr.org/assessment/pdf/Prof_dev_guided.pdf.

Procedure:

1. Provide participants with an article on the role of data analysis. You may use one of the handouts listed or find your own. Keep in mind that you want a piece of writing that clearly links data analysis to instructional planning.
2. Ask participants to mark their copy of the article as they read, highlighting words, phrases, or concepts from the text that they find the most meaningful and personally relevant.
3. Pause for a 10-minute pair-and-share conversation in which participants turn to a partner and share their reactions to the article.
4. Ask participants to continue reading the article and marking meaningful words, phrases, or concepts.
5. Pause for another 10-minute pair-and-share.
6. Have each pair join another pair (to form groups of four) to "report out" their understanding of the article content.
7. Facilitate a whole-group discussion of data analysis for instructional planning and its implications for literacy coaching.

Module 6
Jigsaw of Study Group Formats

Time: 2 hours
Participants: Literacy coaches, administrators, and teachers

Purpose:

- To introduce selected study group formats and strategies.
- To highlight attributes of study groups that contribute to professional learning.
- To inform participants about helpful resources on the topic of study groups.
- To provide participants with the opportunity to work in a collaborative group on a common focus.

Materials Needed:

- Information on selected study group formats (see the Resource List at the end of this module)
- Chart paper, markers, and tape

Procedure:

1. Divide participants into jigsaw groups with no more than four people in each group.

2. Give each jigsaw group a prepared packet of materials on a study group format. The packet might include (a) a fact sheet on the format, (b) additional materials you have collected from online resources, and (c) other items that you want the group to review.

3. Have each group determine how they will study the materials on their assigned format (e.g., "jigsaw" the article and then share with other team members, read the article aloud within small groups and then note the important content on chart paper) and then ask them to review the materials.

4. Ask the group members to think about the best way to share information with their colleagues. You may wish to use the following key questions to guide their planning:
   • What are the main features of this model?
   • Why do you think this model would be effective?
   • What do you think are some of the challenges of this format?
   • Describe a circumstance when you might recommend one of these study group methods.
   • How could this model be incorporated into your school's professional learning plan?

5. Have each group present their findings to their colleagues.

6. Close the session by giving each participant a copy of the handouts for all selected study group formats.

Resource List
Lesson Study Format

The Research for Better Schools Web site: www.rbs.org

"Lesson Study: Japanese Method Benefits All Teachers" by Joan Richardson (2001). Available on the Web site of the National Staff Development Council: www.nsdc. org/library/publications/results/res12-00rich.cfm

Teachers College, Columbia University–Lesson Study Research Group Web site: www. tc.edu/lessonstudy/worksamples.html

Data Dialogues Format

"Lead Data Dialogues: Examining Your Monitoring Data" by the Maryland Department of Education (n.d.) Available on the department's Web site: www.mdk12.org/data/course/m4w3/pr3/

Leadership Folio Series: Sustaining School Improvement by Mid-continent Research for Education and Learning (n.d.). Available on the organization's Web site: www.mcrel.org/PDF/LeadershipOrganizationDevelopment/5031TG_datafolio.pdf

Critical Friends Format

"How Friends Can Be Critical as Schools Make Essential Change" by Kathleen Cushman (1998). Available on the Web site of the Coalition of Essential Schools: www.essentialschools.org/cs/resources/view/ces_res/43

Critical Friends Groups: Frequently Asked Questions by the staff of the National School Reform Faculty (2006). Available on the organization's Web site: www.nsrfharmony.org/faq.html#1

"Having 'Another Set of Eyeballs': Critical Friends Groups" by staff of the Northwest Regional Educational Laboratory (NWREL). (2005). Available on NWREL's Web site: www.nwrel.org/nwedu/11-01/cfg/

Looking at Student Work Format

"Looking Collaboratively at Student Work: An Essential Toolkit" by Kathleen Cushman (1996). Available on the Web site of the Coalition of Essential Schools: www.essentialschools.org/cs/resources/view/ces_res/57

Tools, an online article the Web site of the Small Schools Project (n.d.): http://smallschoolsproject.org/index.asp?siteloc=tool&section=guidelines

Case Studies

"Teaching Materials Using Case Studies" by Claire Davis and Elizabeth Wilcock (2006). Available on the Web site of the Higher Education Academy: www.materials.ac.uk/guides/casestudies.asp

Happy Accidents: Cases as Opportunities for Teacher Learning by Judith H. Shulman (2002). Available on the WestED Web site: www.wested.org/online_pubs/happyaccidents.pdf

Module 7
Literacy Program Inventory

Time: Variable, depending on the information collection method
Participants: Literacy coaches, administrators, and teachers

Purpose:

- To help participants gather baseline information about their literacy program by taking inventories of assessments, curriculum materials, and human resources.
- To use the information from the inventory surveys to identify gaps, patterns of usage, and overlaps, so as to streamline processes.

Materials Needed:

- Handout: Template for an Assessment Inventory (Figure M7-A)
- Handout: Template for an Instructional Materials Inventory (Figure M7-B)
- Handout: Template for a Human Resources Inventory (Figure M7-C)
- Charts, presentation slides, or overhead transparencies showing the purpose for each inventory

---

Purpose of an Assessment Inventory

- To identify what assessment instruments the school currently uses.
- To identify gaps in the school's literacy assessment process.
- To help the school develop a common vision for assessment practice.

Purpose of an Instructional Materials Inventory

- To identify which instructional programs and materials the school currently uses.
- To reflect on how the school uses these programs and materials.
- To document material availability, usage, and gaps in the school's instructional processes.

Purpose of a Human Resources Inventory

- To identify the school literacy program's *internal human resources* (e.g., librarian, reading specialist, technology support staff).
- To identify the school literacy program's *external human resources* (e.g., district personnel, external vendors or consultants, volunteer reading coaches).
- To identify gaps in the literacy services available.
- To determine whether the school staff is making the best use of the human resources available.

Procedure:

Note: Unless otherwise noted, the procedure is the same for all three inventories: Assessment, Instructional Materials, and Human Resources.

1. Give participants copies of the inventory documents.
2. Review the overhead slides that outline the purpose of each inventory.

For the Human Resources Inventory, additional points to cover include the following:

- This inventory also provides the opportunity to collect
    - Information about schedules for external and internal human resources.

Figure M7-A   Template for an Assessment Inventory

DOWNLOAD

- *Screening Assessments* identify students who are lagging behind in growth of critical skills.
- *Formative Assessments* monitor growth of all students' critical reading skills for the purpose of informing instructional planning.
- *Diagnostic Assessments* identify specific skill deficiencies characteristic of identified reading disorders.
- *Outcome Assessments* measure the critical elements of reading growth at the end of an instructional year; typically, they help teachers determine if the child is on track to read on grade level by grade X.

Directions: Please fill in the names or a brief description of assessments you currently use.

Current Screening Assessments:

Current Formative Assessments:

Current Diagnostic Assessments:

Current Outcome Assessments:

– Job descriptions of the positions relevant to literacy instruction support.

– Information about how other schools and districts are maximizing their staff through creative staffing patterns.

• This inventory may help resolve questions such as

– Do we have sufficient staff? If not, who are we missing?

– Are we making the best use of the staff that we do have?

– Are we thinking outside of the box in terms of how we use our internal and external human resources?

– Does our current schedule result in the best coverage?

– Do our current human resources equip us to provide the services our students need to succeed? What is the evidence of a tiered instructional response system (Tier I = regular classroom instruction, Tier II = supplemental instruction, and Tier III = special education)?

– What professional learning supports are in place to support our staff?

– Are we fully exploring our options and establishing practices to "grow our own" local experts over the long haul?

3. Walk through an example with the participants.

4. Divide the participants into small working groups. Each group should complete a form, and the resulting information can then be compiled into a master sheet.

5. After collecting the information, lead a discussion of the implications of the data. Keep the discussion focused by revisiting the purposes of each inventory.

Figure M7-B   Template for an
Instructional Materials Inventory

DOWNLOAD

Directions: Please fill in the names and descriptive information of the materials you currently use.

Instructional Materials Title:

Description:

Stated Purpose and Grade Level:

Assessment Components:

Literacy Components:

1. Describe the material's interest level and potential to engage students.

2. How do you currently use the material?

3. How do you intend to use the material?

4. Does the product build teachers' expertise about effective reading instruction? If so, in what way?

DOWNLOAD

Figure M7-C   Template for a
Human Resources Inventory

Directions: Please fill in the names and related information on literacy support personal currently available.

Internal Resources:

Title:

Role: Availability:

Title:

Role: Availability:

Title:

Role: Availability:

External Resources:

Title:

Role: Availability:

Title:

Role: Availability:

Title:

Role: Availability:

Module 8
The Demonstration Lesson: Planning Meeting

Time: 30 minutes

Participants: Literacy coaches and teachers

Purpose:

- To model the process of preparing for a demonstration lesson.
- To engage coaches and teachers in reflective conversations about demonstration lessons and their potential implications for instructional growth.
- To engage coaches and teachers in reflective conversations about literacy learning and instructional practices.

Materials Needed:

- Handout: Worksheet for Planning a Demonstration Lesson (Figure M8)
- Handout: Chapter 8: Demonstration Lessons
- Chart, presentation slide, or overhead transparency providing an overview of the purpose of demonstration lessons

---

The Purpose of Demonstration Lessons

• To model teaching methods, strategies, or content to teachers who are less familiar or confident with them.
• To provide a common experience of teaching that will be the basis for discussing and developing practice.
• To foster self-reflection and creative problem solving.

Remember: The demonstration lesson must have a clear focus and be aligned to the coaching program's articulated goals and objectives.

Procedure:

1. Review the purpose of demonstration lessons using the recommended definition. You might also refer to Chapter 8 for additional information.

2. Set up the room with a table for the demonstration lesson team and a semicircle of chairs for the observation group.

3. Assemble the demonstration lesson team, consisting of the teacher who will be observing the demonstration lesson and the primary literacy coach (or the coach facilitator) who will be teaching the demonstration lesson. Other coaches observing this conversation as part of their professional learning constitute the "fishbowl" group. They can alternate teaching the demonstration lesson at subsequent sessions.

4. Using the Worksheet for Planning a Demonstration Lesson (Figure M8), the primary coach engages the teacher in conversation about the lesson to be demonstrated, covering the following steps:

   – Determine coaching goals.
   – Review the lesson to be observed.
   – Discuss the focus of the observation.
   – Agree on formats for collecting information for subsequent discussion.

5. Consider asking the coaches in the fishbowl to focus on a specific aspect of the planning meeting that aligns with their professional learning goals. For example, if coaches are learning how to use open-ended prompts to encourage conversation, this might be the target for their observation of the planning meeting.

6. If you are demonstrating a technique or a process (such as guided reading), it is helpful for the primary coach to share with everyone involved a protocol that outlines the steps involved in the procedure. (See Appendix C for a sample protocol for guided reading.) This protocol can help focus the conversation during the lesson's debriefing session.

7. Proceed to the classroom for the demonstration lesson.

DOWNLOAD

Figure M8   Worksheet
for Planning a Demonstration Lesson

Learning Standard(s) Addressed:

Focus Area:

Supporting Data:

Coaching Goal(s):

Description of the Lesson to Be Demonstrated:

Focus Questions for the Observing Teacher:

Module 9
The Demonstration Lesson: Debriefing Session

Time: 30 minutes

Participants: Literacy coaches

Purpose:

- To model the process of discussing a demonstration lesson in the debriefing session.
- To engage coaches in reflective conversations about the debriefing component of the demonstration lesson and the implications for instructional growth.
- To engage coaches in reflective conversation about literacy learning and instructional practices.

Materials Needed:

- Completed version of the Worksheet for Planning a Demonstration Lesson (see Figure M8) used for the demonstration lesson
- Any support materials that might inform the discussion, such as Appendix C's framework for guided reading
- Handout: Steps for Discussing a Demonstration Lesson (see Figure M9)

Procedure:

1. Set up the room so that the primary coach (who demonstrated the lesson) and the teacher-observer sit together and the other coaches are in the "fishbowl," monitoring but not participating in the debriefing session. They may record their observations of the conversation for later discussion.

2. The primary coach and the teacher use the lesson planning template (and any other support documents) to guide their discussion, covering the following steps:

   − Revisit instructional focus and coaching goal.
   − Discuss highlights.
   − Review information the teacher collected while observing the demonstration lesson.
   − Ask and respond to questions that came up.

3. The primary coach uses the prompts in the Steps for Discussing a Demonstration Lesson handout (see Figure M9) to guide the conversation.

4. The primary coach and the teacher determine the next step of action planning, which might include one or more of the following:

   − Teacher and coach coplan an extension lesson.
   − Teacher and coach coteach an extension lesson.
   − Teacher incorporates components of demonstration lesson into practice.
   − Coach observes teacher presenting lesson with the same focus.
   − Coach plans a minilesson based on the instructional focus to clarify or extend knowledge.

5. As an extension of this activity, you might suggest a study group on the topic of facilitating collegial conversations. Refer interested parties to *Literacy Coaching: Developing Effective Teachers Through Instructional Dialogue* (Duncan, 2006).

Figure M9   Steps for Discussing a Demonstration Lesson

These steps can provide a structure for a literacy coach's discussion of a demonstration lesson with teachers. Use one or more of the prompts provided for each step, depending on the focus of the conversation and the teacher's response.

1. **Discuss the relationship between the demonstration lesson's purpose and procedure and the teacher's current teaching practice.**
   - How is this lesson like lessons that you teach?
   - How could you use this kind of lesson with your students?
   - How does this kind of lesson fit in with your current teaching practice?

2. **Discuss the lesson overall and ask the teacher to address any points that stood out.**
   - Do you have any questions about this lesson?
   - Did anything you noticed in this lesson surprise you?
   - Did this lesson confirm any specific ideas that you have about learning?

3. **Highlight one specific teaching point of the demonstration lesson as a way to reflect on instructional decision making.**
   - Provide an example of a specific student response to instruction. *Example:* "Did you notice when Mary asked for help?"
   - Highlight the demonstration teacher's response to the student behavior. *Example:* "Mr. Gee told her to reread. Why do you think he chose to do this?"
   - Share the thinking of the coach and the demonstration teacher.
   - Discuss the student's response to the teacher's action and what could be inferred about student learning. *Example:* "Then Mary identified the word. Why do you think this happened?"
   - Share the thinking of the coach and the demonstration teacher.
   - Relate this example to teacher practice. *Example:* "How could you use this strategy to help your students?"

4. **Highlight a second specific teaching point of the demonstration lesson.**

5. **Discuss how the teacher might use what he or she learned from the demonstration lesson.**
   - What kinds of things did you see in this lesson that you are thinking of trying?
   - What kinds of things could you do to build on this lesson?
   - What do you think students learned from this lesson?

Source: Developed by Elizabeth Powers and used with permission.

Module 10
The Demonstration Lesson:
Discussing the Debriefing Session

Time: 1 hour

Participants: The coach who conducted a demonstration lesson debriefing, coaches who observed the process, and a facilitator (coach trainer, lead coach, coach supervisor)

Purpose:

• To give the coaches an opportunity to reflect on the debriefing discussion that they observed between the primary coach (who demonstrated the lesson) and the teacher.

• To highlight key components of the debriefing discussion.

Materials Needed: None

Procedure:

1. Ask the participants to discuss the following questions in pairs:

   – How does the discussion of the demonstration lesson (the debriefing discussion) support the work that you do?

   – How is the discussion like the ones you have with teachers you coach?

   – How could you use this kind of discussion with teachers?

2. Review the general structure and content of the debriefing discussion. Ask the participants if they have any questions, noticed anything surprising, or noticed anything that confirmed their ideas and beliefs about coaching.

3. Provide an example of one specific point the coach made during the coaching conversation, and then discuss with participants the teacher's response to the point and the coach's interaction with the teacher about that point. Be sure to discuss the coach's purpose for the interaction and what can be inferred about teacher understanding and learning.

4. Repeat Step 3 with a second point from the coaching conversation.

5. Ask participants to consider how they can use what they learned from this example. How might the debriefing discussion have helped a teacher to reflect on her understanding of effective instruction or of student learning? What techniques did participants see that they might use? What new ideas do they have about their coaching?

6. Summarize key points to review at subsequent meetings.

Module 11

Evaluating Professional Learning:
Exploring Points of View

Time: 1 hour

Participants: Literacy coaches, administrators, and teachers

Purpose:

- To explore two frameworks for evaluating professional development—one from Thomas Guskey of the University of Kentucky and the other from Joellen Killion of the National Staff Development Council.
- To introduce participants to protocols that can be used to design an evaluation of professional learning.

Materials Needed:

- Handout: "Questions and Answers: A Conversation with Thomas Guskey," an article published in the Harvard Family Research Project's (2005/2006) online newsletter *The Evaluation Exchange* (Available: www.gse.harvard.edu/hfrp/eval/issue32/qanda.html).
- Handout: "Evaluating the Impact of Professional Development in Eight Steps," an article by Joellen Killion (2005/2006) published in the same issue of *The Evaluation Exchange* (www.gse.harvard.edu/hfrp/eval/issue32/spotlight1.html).

Procedure:

1. Divide the group into two teams of four members each. If there are more than eight session participants, ask two or more teams to focus on each protocol (i.e., two teams would look at the Killion model and two would look at the Guskey model).

2. Share information with participants about the importance of evaluating the connection between educators' professional learning and student achievement. Reviewing Chapter 2 will help you to facilitate this.

3. Explain that in this activity, they will have an opportunity to learn about two evaluation protocols: The Eight Step Process, articulated by Joellen Killion, and the Five Levels of Evaluation by Thomas Guskey.

4. Distribute the articles and ask participants to highlight the key components of the model as they read. They should be prepared to share the information with their colleagues.

5. Lead a discussion with participants about the models, comparing and contrasting their methods and points of view.

6. For an extension activity, ask each participant to choose one of the models for further independent study. Two additional resources that might be helpful are Guskey's *Evaluating Professional Development* (2000) and Killion's *Assessing Impact* (2002).

Module 12
Preparing for a Focused Classroom Visit

Time: 1 hour

Participants: Literacy coaches, administrators, and teachers

Purpose:

- To point out the difference in the quality of a reflective conversation that takes place after a focused classroom visit compared with an unstructured visit.
- To give the participants practice in taking focused notes during an observation.
- To review the purposes of a focused classroom visit.

Materials Needed:

- Video clip of a literacy classroom (Hildi Perez's 1st grade class) from *Teaching Reading: Assessment Driven Instruction.* This video on demand is available from Annenberg Media Web site at www.learner.org/channel/libraries/readingk2/perez/index.html.
- Handout: Appendix C: Sample Protocol for a Literacy Process
- Chart paper and markers

Procedure:

1. Show a video of a guided reading lesson (from *Teaching Reading: Assessment Driven Instruction,* or a vignette of your choosing) and ask participants to take notes on what they observe.

2. Discuss and record their observations on the chart paper. Set aside notations for later discussion.

3. Distribute and review the Sample Protocol for a Literacy Process (Appendix C), which provides a framework for a guided reading lesson.

4. Show the video a second time, asking the participants to focus on the instructional goal of improving the child's comprehension and to observe for *prompts that the teacher gives to encourage use of the text comprehension strategy.*

5. Record on the chart participants' observations related to the focus (prompts for strategy use) and discuss.

6. Ask the participants to compare the notes from the two discussions—an unstructured observation as compared to a focused observation.

7. Highlight the value of having a clear focus when observing classroom practice.

Module 13
Carousel Brainstorming on Focused Classroom Visits

Time: 1 hour

Participants: Literacy coaches

Purpose:

• To tap participants' prior knowledge about focused classroom visits.

• To encourage an exchange of perspectives.

• To generate recommendations from the group to review for possible implementation.

Materials Needed:

• Chart paper and markers (one color per team)

• The Questions for Discussion from Chapter 5 (see p. 57)

Procedure:

This exercise is designed to identify the collective thinking of a group in a nonevaluative environment. Using this format, groups "carousel" around the room, rotating among questions.

1. Write each of Chapter 5's Questions for Discussion at the top of the sheets of chart paper, and tape the questions on the walls, allowing ample room around each chart so groups can converge around them.
2. Divide the participants into teams and give each team a different colored marker.
3. Assign a role to each group member (e.g., recorder, encourager, monitor, speaker).
4. Establish a time limit to complete the assigned question.
5. Ask each group to discuss its ideas and responses to the question. Responses are written down on the chart by the recorder.
6. After the time limit, rotate the groups. Make sure the group carries its marker to the next question. However, be sure to rotate the role of the recorder. Groups cannot reiterate previously stated responses, but they can continue to add new ideas to the list.
7. Repeat the procedure for the remaining questions until the cycle is complete.
8. Post the charts in the front of the room and ask each group to discuss how the information and ideas were elicited. For each question, rotate the role of speaker within each group. A recorder from each group writes down all the responses listed for its initial question.
9. Make copies of the responses and distribute them to the participants.
10. As an extension activity, ask the participants to write a position statement on the issue.

Note: This activity could be conducted with any of this book's chapter-specific Questions for Discussion. You might also generate a set of custom questions based on local needs.

Module 14
Defining a Coaching "Theory of Change" and "Theory of Action"

Time: 2 hours

Participants: Literacy coaches, administrators, and teachers

Purpose:

- To define the terms *theory of change* and *theory of action*.
- To give administrators, coaches, and teachers the opportunity to think about their own coaching theory of change and theory of action.

Materials Needed:

- Chart paper and markers
- Handout: "Evaluations to Watch: Theory of Action in Practice," an article by Claudia Weisburd and Tamara Sniad (2005/2006) available at www.gse.harvard.edu/hfrp/eval/issue32/eval3.html
- Handout: *The Spokane School District: Intentionally Building Capacity That Leads to Increased Student Achievement: Theory of Action,* an article by Susan E. Sather (2004), available on the NWREL Web site. www.nwrcl.org/scpd/re-engineering/SpokaneSD/TheoryAction.asp

- Handout: *A Theory of Action for High School Reform: A Conversation with Alan Bersin,* a report to the Carnegie Corporation of New York (2006), available online at www.publicengagement.com/practices/publications/documents/bersin.pdf
- Handout: *Theory of Action,* an online piece by Partners in School Innovation (n.d.), available at www.partnersinschools.org/program/theory.html
- Overhead transparencies or presentation slides that define theory of change and theory of action:

Definitions

- A *theory of change* identifies the philosophy or theory that informs a given type of change you want to occur.
- A *theory of action* maps out your specific pathway to reaching the change or changes you want to occur.

Procedure:

1. On chart paper, write the terms *theory of change* and *theory of action.*
2. Ask participants to jot down their personal understanding of what the terms mean.
3. Write some of the key points on the chart paper.
4. Hand out the sample documents and ask participants to summarize the theory of change and the theory of action for each of the samples.
5. Determine attributes of each type of theory.
6. Discuss the question "What do we believe about coaching?" and write responses on chart paper.
7. Ask participants to respond to the following question with their colleagues: "What is our theory of change and our theory of action for *our* coaching program?"
8. At a follow-up meeting, ask the coaches to discuss the implications of the articulated theory of change and theory of action for their coaching program.

Module 15
"Change" Versus "Evolving Practice"

Time: 1 hour

Participants: Literacy coaches

Purpose:

• To give coaches the opportunity to talk about change.

• To provide time to reflect on the implications of change for their coaching practice.

Materials Needed:

• Handout: The Change Process as It Applies to Coaching (Figure M15)

Procedure:

1. Hand out copies of The Change Process as It Applies to Coaching.
2. Ask participants to read the essay and respond to the questions at the end.
3. Ask participants to "pair and share."
4. Lead a group discussion about the participants' reactions and responses.

Figure M15   The Change Process
As It Applies to Coaching

Why is the topic of "change" an essential and initial component of the professional learning provided to the coach?

It starts with the coaches themselves. Many of you come to the job with a background in teaching. You are accustomed to having your own classroom, working side by side with colleagues on equal footing, perhaps in the same school where you teach. As a literacy coach, the lens through which your colleagues view you has changed. You continue to view them as teaching colleagues (indeed they are), but they may wonder why you are the coach, what you will make them do, or what you will no longer permit them to do. This is change personified.

As you adjust to your new position, you will be asked to support others as they evolve in their practice. (They will also be a support to you as you evolve in your practice.) As one would expect, some people will respond with enthusiasm, and others will wonder why things can't stay the way they were. You may be viewed as the instigator of trouble to come! For teachers who are used to a diet of "drive-by workshops," the transition to job-embedded professional learning can be challenging.

The Literacy Coaching Continuum assumes that your teaching colleagues will be involved in choosing their own path for professional learning—that they will be provided with ongoing opportunities for reflection, and that you, as the coach, will be available to them as a supportive colleague.

I recommend that you *not* think of teachers who aren't keen on the idea of coaching as "resistors." Just using the term to describe people in this way sets up an adversarial relationship. The fact is that not everyone will embrace coaching. It *should* be a choice.

This doesn't mean that teachers are not expected to evolve in their practice. This doesn't mean that teachers are not expected to teach a rigorous and relevant curriculum. This doesn't mean that students are not expected to achieve to high standards.

It does mean that coaching is offered as one way to support teachers as their practice evolves, whether they are novice or seasoned. Coaching is an option that is part of the negotiation between the teachers and the administrators of the school, not between the coach and the teacher.

In the sporting world, having a coach is a given. The caliber of the coach is seen as pivotal to the success of the individual and team. In the business world, coaching is viewed as a sign of success. One engages a coach to increase success, not to mark those who aren't successful. In education, coaching is still viewed by many as a remedial service. What impact does this attitude have on coaching? What can you do to alter this attitude? How do your coaching program policies add to or dispel this perspective?

Module 16
Celebrating Success Quick-Write

Time: 1 hour

Participants: Literacy coaches

Purpose:

- To celebrate success as a support strategy to maintain momentum and focus on positive strategies for coaching.
- To make transparent the connection between coaching action and the resulting success.
- To give literacy coaches time to reflect on a successful experience.
- To give literacy coaches the opportunity to share their success with their colleagues.
- To build a collection of experiences that can be used to record group experience. These can be shared with new coaches or used to document growth over time.

Materials Needed:

- Overhead transparency or presentation slide that provides the following Quick-Write guidelines:

Quick-Write

1. Describe a situation that you think of as a coaching success.
2. Which actions of yours contributed to this success?
3. Which actions by the teacher or teachers coached contributed to this success?
4. Is the connection between the steps taken and the success experienced clear to both you and the teacher or teachers you coached? If not, how might you clarify this connection?

Procedure:

1. Ask participants to spend about 10 minutes writing about one of their coaching successes, using the prepared Quick-Write prompts as a guide. They might write about a particular coaching interaction with a teacher, a professional learning format that was established (such as regular study groups), or anything else that they feel they accomplished during their coaching year.
2. After the 10-minute Quick-Write, ask the participants to turn to a partner and share the experience they wrote about.
3. Lead a discussion about the importance of regularly celebrating success.

APPENDIXES

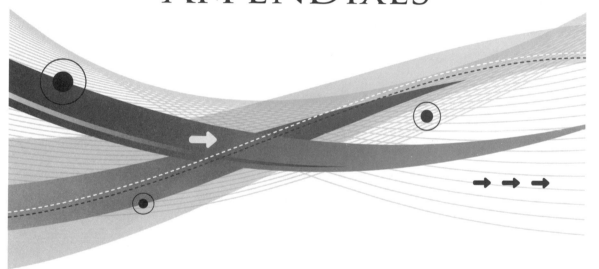

Appendix A

Job Criteria and Professional Learning

Job Criteria for Literacy Coaches

In the publication *The Role and Qualifications of the Reading Coach in the United States* (2004), the International Reading Association (IRA) suggests the following criteria:

> The Reading Coach
> 1. Must be an excellent classroom teacher;
> 2. Must have in-depth knowledge of reading processes, acquisition, assessment, and instruction;
> 3. Must have experience working with teachers to improve their practice;
> 4. Must be an excellent presenter and be familiar with presenting to teacher groups in the contexts of schools and at professional conferences at the local, state, and even national levels. Reading coaches should also be skilled in leading teacher groups to facilitate reflection and change for their colleagues;
> 5. Must have experience or preparation that enables them to master the complexities of observing and modeling in classrooms and providing feedback to teachers, and be able to develop trusting relationships with teachers in order to serve effectively in a coaching role. (pp. 3–4)

In 2005, the IRA (2006a) surveyed reading and literacy coaches to learn what qualifications were required for their positions. According to the 140 respondents, a B.A. and a teaching certificate were the only clear requirements. Fewer than half reported that they needed an M.A., and only 19 percent indicated that an M.A. in literacy or a related area was required. The survey also asked coaches about their roles and responsibilities. You may download a full report of the findings at www.reading. org/resources/issues/focus_coaching.html.

In the February/March 2006 issue of the IRA publication *Reading Today*, Richard L. Allington points out the paradox of our current system: we hope student achievement will increase, yet we fail to ensure that only qualified personnel (reading specialists, reading teachers, and reading coaches) will provide the support services needed. To meet the standard of qualification, a reading specialist credential *should* be required for anyone assuming the position of literacy coach.

Ongoing Professional Learning for Literacy Coaches

In addition to preparation at the preservice level, ongoing and job-embedded professional learning for coaches is a critical feature of an effective coaching program.

In 2006, Florida became the first state to form a statewide association for literacy coaches. The Florida Literacy Coaches Association was "created through a partnership between a select group of literacy coaches from around the state and the Just Read, Florida! office." Their mission is to unite "literacy coaches to support and advocate for the literacy needs of all stakeholders in schools across Florida." They have published a *Position Statement on the Roles and Qualifications of Literacy Coaches in Florida* that can be downloaded from their Web site at www.justreadflorida.com/FLCA/.

This information might inspire you to start a similar group in your state or region. An association can serve to galvanize discussions to inform practice and guide policy development, while providing much-needed local support to those who assume the role of literacy coach.

Appendix B

Contact Information and Resources for Coaching Models

Author's note: This list is not all-inclusive. I have included various models and programs that provide helpful resources on their Web sites. I'm always interested in hearing about coaching programs. If you are part of or know about others, please contact me at mcmoran@escort.org or marycatherine.moran@gmail.com.

Program	Contact Information	Read More About It
After-School Literacy Coaching Initiative (LCI)	Boston's After-School for All Partnership 245 Summer Street, Suite 1401 Boston, MA 02210 Phone: 617-624-8133	www.mass2020.org/projects.lci.html
Alabama Reading First Initiative (ARFI)	ARFI Education Specialists Alabama Reading First Initiative Phone: 334-353-1570	www.alsde.edu/html/sections/section_detail.asp?section=90&footer=sections
Arkansas Comprehensive Literacy Model	Dr. Linda Dorn University of Arkansas at Little Rock 2801 South University Avenue Little Rock, AR 72204-1099 Phone: 501-569-8613	www.arliteracymodel.com

Program	Contact Information	Read More About It
Bellingham School District Model of Developing Coaches	Bellingham Public Schools 1306 Dupont Street Bellingham, WA 98225-3198 Phone: 360-647-6800	http://www.bham.wednet.edu/departments/currdpt/profdev/pddistlearnfac.htm
Collaborative Coaching and Learning (CCL)	Boston Plan for Excellence 6 Beacon Street #615 Boston, MA 02108 Phone: 617-227-8055	www.bpe.org/
Content-Focused Coaching in Elementary Literacy	Donna DiPrima Bickel, Chair Institute for Learning 310 LRDC 3939 O'Hara Street University of Pittsburgh Pittsburgh, PA 15260 Phone: 412-624-8319	www.institutefor learning.org
Every Child a Reader & Writer Initiative	Noyce Foundation 2500 El Camino Real, Suite 110 Palo Alto, CA 94306 Phone: 650-856-2600	www.noycefdn.org/literacy/index.html
Just Read, Florida! The Florida Reading Coach Model	Just Read, Florida! 325 West Gaines Street, Suite 1548 Tallahassee, FL 32399 Phone: 850-245-0503	www.justreadflorida.com
Literacy Collaborative	Literacy Collaborative Program Ohio State University 807 Kinnear Road Columbus, OH 43212 Phone: 800-678-6486	www.lcosu.org
Pathways to Success—Instructional Coaching: Progress Through Partnership	The University of Kansas Center for Research on Learning Joseph R. Pearson Hall 1122 West Campus Road, Room 521 Lawrence, KS 66045-3101 Phone: 785-864-4780	www.ku-crl.org
Pennsylvania High School Coaching Initiative	Pennsylvania High School Coaching Initiative Moorestown West Corporate Center 2 Executive Drive, Suite 1 Moorestown, NJ 08057 Phone: 856-533-1645	http://pacoaching.org

Program	Contact Information	Read More About It
The South Carolina Reading Initiative (SCRI)	South Carolina Department of Education 1429 Senate Street Columbia, SC 29201 Phone: 803-734-6102	http://ed.sc.gov/
Spokane Public Schools Professional Learning Model	Director, Professional Learning Spokane School District No. 81 200 N. Bernard Street Spokane, WA 99201 Phone: 509-354-5900	www.spokaneschools.org/ProfessionalLearning/Initiatives/InstructionalCoaching/IC.stm
Springboard Schools (formerly Bay Area School Reform Collaboration)	Springboard Schools 181 Fremont Street, 2nd Floor San Francisco, CA 94105 Phone: 415-348-5500	www.springboardschools.org

Sample Protocol for a Literacy Process

A Framework for a Guided Reading Lesson

Framework Component	Teacher Action	Teacher Observations
Selecting the Text	Texts and strategies are not determined by grade level. Text selection always leaves some "reading work" for the child to do. Choose an "instructional-level text" or one that children can read with the assistance of a teacher, tutor, or capable other with an accuracy rate of 90 to 95 percent. Read the book before class time. As you read, consider the following questions, always keeping the students in mind: • What skills can be taught with this book? • What connections can the students make when reading this book? Text to self? ("I have a car like the one in the book.") Text to text? ("This reminds me of that other book we read.") Text to world? ("I saw one of those when I visited my granny.") • What prior observations about the students should be factored into the plan for teaching this book? • What material that students encountered in the preceding lesson will be helpful during this lesson? • What modifications/adaptations will be required so that all students can fully access the content?	

Framework Component	Teacher Action	Teacher Observations
Introducing the Book	Read the title and the names of the author and the illustrator. Talk about the cover. Give a one- or two-sentence summary of the book. When planning your book introduction, consider the following questions: • What information will help the students with the text? • What hooks might be used to tap students' prior knowledge? As students prepare to read the book, do the following: • Draw attention to unusual language. • Draw attention to strategy use. • Briefly discuss experiences that may help the students link the book to their own prior experiences.	
Reading the Text	As students read silently at their own pace, rotate among them, guiding their reading efforts in ways designed to help them develop independent reading strategies. Provide prompts as needed.	
Revisiting the Teaching Focus	After students read the text, bring the group together to validate a strategy or demonstrate or model a teaching point, as necessary.	
Extending the Meaning of the Text (optional)	Determine whether there is a manipulative, game, or activity that will reinforce meaning, and use it as appropriate.	
Doing Word Work (optional)	Determine whether there is a manipulative, game, or activity that will reinforce meaning, and use it as appropriate.	
Closing the Lesson	Ask the question, "What did the student learn today?"	

Appendix D

Role-Play Vignettes
for Literacy Coaching

The following vignettes are actual situations that literacy coaches have shared with me during the course of my work. They typify the kinds of difficult questions and concerns that coaches are expected to handle as part of their duties, and coaches can benefit from reviewing these scenarios and role-playing how they would respond.

In the course of a professional learning meeting, I might try to fit in a couple of the vignettes as a group activity at various points in the agenda. Another idea is to feature a "coaching case" at each meeting, with coaches sharing a challenge they have faced and discussing it with colleagues.

Vignette 1

This requires two participants: one to play a teacher and one to play a newly appointed literacy coach.

Teacher: You have heard that your colleague has been appointed the school's new literacy coach. There was an announcement back in the spring that the school would be creating this position, but you weren't sure what this new literacy effort involved or why a literacy coach was needed. Now you have a number of questions for your newly appointed colleague, pertaining to qualifications, role, and responsibility.

• Why were you chosen?

• Why do we need a literacy coach at our school?

• Are you going to evaluate me?

• Why didn't they take the money they are spending on this initiative and give it to the classroom teachers for more books?

Literacy coach: How will you respond to this teacher's concerns?

Vignette 2

This requires three or more participants, with one playing a newly appointed literacy coach and the rest playing skeptical teachers.

Literacy coach: The rumor is that staff members are questioning your role as the "expert" on all things having to do with literacy. In fact, one teacher commented that she has a lot more experience in the classroom than you do. Meet with your critics to discuss the issue of your qualifications.

Vignette 3

This requires two participants: one to play a teacher and another to play a literacy coach.

Teacher: You teach 3rd grade and seek your literacy coach's advice on strategies and materials to use with your English language learners.

Literacy coach: How can you help this teacher provide these students with appropriately differentiated instruction based on data and aligned to learning standards?

Vignette 4

This requires two participants: one to play a frustrated literacy coach and another to play a literacy coaching supervisor or a colleague.

Literacy coach: School starts in three weeks. There's a new principal this year, and you're hoping that she will have a clearer plan than her predecessor did about how to put your skills to work. Last year, you were left to your own devices, working mostly with parents and teaching assistants, and sometimes contributing to professional development sessions. It was frustrating and unfulfilling. How can you change the dynamic?

Literacy coaching supervisor/colleague: What advice would you have for this literacy coach, who is hoping to get on the right footing with a principal and work with teachers in a meaningful way?

Vignette 5

This requires two participants: one to play a veteran teacher and one to play a newly appointed literacy coach.

Teacher: You've just learned, at an open staff meeting, that your school will be instituting a literacy coaching program. That may be fine for the teachers who need help, but you're not interested. You've been teaching for 25 years and you know your stuff. Make your concerns known.

Literacy coach: How might you respond to this veteran teacher's concerns, remembering that this conversation is taking place before the entire staff?

Vignette 6

This requires two or more participants, all playing literacy coaches.

Literacy coach #1: You're beginning to feel like all you do is demonstration lessons. Teachers are eager for you to come into their classrooms to teach a lesson, but they aren't keen on the idea of engaging in any other professional learning formats. You're also not sure if they understand the purpose of the demonstration lessons. You notice that some of the teachers seem preoccupied when you're doing the teaching, and they don't have much to say at the debrief sessions.

Other coaches: What questions might you ask to clarify your colleague's concerns? How might you respond to your colleague?

Vignette 7

This requires two or more participants, all playing literacy coaches.

Literacy coach #1: You learned during your training that every classroom observation should have a clear focus, but you're finding it hard to find the time to do all this planning. Now, teachers are asking you to pop in and observe. Would it be OK to do this? Yours is a small, friendly staff, and you know they are looking for ideas in their classrooms. Make your case to a group of literacy coach colleagues.

Other literacy coaches: What do you think? How might you respond to your colleague's questions and concerns?

Vignette 8

This requires two or more participants, all playing literacy coaches.

Literacy coach #1: You're frustrated. The teachers haven't even taken the core curriculum materials out of the boxes. You want to work toward a clear focus, but how can you do that when the teachers haven't even taken the first step? Share your concerns with your literacy coach colleagues.

Other literacy coaches: What advice do you have for your colleague?

Vignette 9

This requires two participants: one to play a principal and the other to play a literacy coach.

Principal: The literacy coach position is a new one, and you need to figure out how to communicate with your school's literacy coach to assess how things are going. Talk to your literacy coach about how the two of you can make time to review the program on a regular basis.

Literacy coach: What ideas do you have? Alternatively, pretend it is you who must initiate this conversation with your principal. How might you approach it?

Vignette 10

This requires two participants: one to play a literacy coach and the other to play a teacher.

Literacy coach: You were invited into a classroom to observe a teacher's guided reading lesson. As the lesson progressed, you realized that the teacher did not seem to understand what guided reading is, or understand the purpose of this instructional grouping format. (The students read a predictable text, round-robin style, and the teacher stopped after each reading to ask a series of limiting comprehension questions.) Now, you and the teacher are meeting to discuss the observation. How will you clarify what guided reading is and is not? What things can you do the next time around to avoid this situation?

Other literacy coaches: What might your colleague (and you) do next time to avoid this kind of confusion? Given the current situation, do you have any suggestions on how to clarify what guided reading is and is not?

Vignette 11

This requires two or more participants, all playing literacy coaches.

Literacy coach #1: One challenge for you is to find balance between the students' intervention needs and the teacher's needs in implementing a new reading program. And as the year progresses, these needs will evolve! How do you find balance? What's the best schedule? Share your questions and concerns with literacy coach colleagues.

Other literacy coaches: How would you respond to your colleague's questions and concerns? What approaches have worked for you? What advice can you give?

Vignette 12

This requires two or more participants, all playing literacy coaches.

Literacy coach #1: Several of the teachers at your school are highly skilled veterans who have figured out "what works for them." You've tried to introduce them to some new strategies—approaches you believe would really benefit their students—but they're not interested. Share your concerns with literacy coach colleagues.

Other literacy coaches: How would you respond to your colleague's situation? What approaches have worked for you? What advice can you give?

Vignette 13

This requires two or more participants, all playing literacy coaches.

Literacy coach #1: Teachers at your school aren't sure they can trust you, your literacy coaching approach, or the whole idea of literacy coaching. They felt the reading program they had was pretty good and didn't need to be replaced. What do you do now?

Other literacy coaches: How would you respond to your colleague's situation? What advice can you give?

Appendix E

End-of-Year Review for a Literacy Coaching Program

An end-of-year review gives literacy coaches and coordinating administrators an opportunity to think about the actions taken throughout the school year and helps to clarify what the program's focus should be in the year to come.

Directions:

1. Fill out the cover sheet. Make sure to list all of your team members and include all of the requested information.

2. Review the five component categories critical to a sound literacy program: Coaching, Assessment, Data Analysis, Intervention Strategies, and Support Networks. For each category, review the indicators and decide if you have taken any steps toward achieving them. If the answer is yes, decide if you are in the beginning, emerging, systematic, or sustainable phase. (Refer to the sample form on p. 172 if you need guidance.) In the box under the appropriate header, list some concrete examples of what you are doing. If you need more room, use the back of the sheet. Be sure to include the component and the indicator to make clear what the additional information applies to.

Keep in mind that you are not expected to be working on all of these indicators at the same time.

Literacy Program
End-of-Year Review

DOWNLOAD

Date: _____

School: _____

District: _____

Review Team Members:

Name　　　　　　　　　　　　**Position**　　　　　　　**E-mail**

Source: Developed by M. C. Moran and Michele Sloan-Cheney. Used with permission.

Program Components

1. Coaching—The literacy coach provides assistance to teachers at individual and group levels to ensure implementation of literacy professional learning components to promote effective instruction.

Indicator	Beginning (B)	Emerging (E)	Systematic (S)	Sustainable (SS)
a. Our literacy coach facilitates, coaches, mentors, and presents information that meets the needs and skill level of the individual or groups of teachers.				
b. Our literacy coach conducts focused dialogue at the individual, grade, school, or district level to promote knowledge and build skills in assessment, diagnosis, data analysis, interventions, etc.				

1. Coaching (continued)

Indicator	Beginning (B)	Emerging (E)	Systematic (S)	Sustainable (SS)
c. Our literacy coach supports teachers as they try new strategies and techniques.				
d. Our literacy coach helps teachers with ongoing assessment and analysis of data.				
e. Our literacy coach gives feedback based on observations, conversations, student work/data, questions, or teacher requests within the adopted curriculum.				

Indicator	Beginning (B)	Emerging (E)	Systematic (S)	Sustainable (SS)
f. Our literacy coach regularly schedules structured study teams focused on reading.				

2. Assessment—What we know or have learned about the individual student's literacy-related strengths and challenges.

Indicator	Beginning (B)	Emerging (E)	Systematic (S)	Sustainable (SS)
a. Our teachers know what needs to be assessed in reading for all children, including ELLs, students with disabilities, and other special populations.				

2. Assessment (continued)

Indicator	Beginning (B)	Emerging (E)	Systematic (S)	Sustainable (SS)
b. Our teachers know how to use formal and informal assessments to identify strengths and challenges for all students.				
c. Our teachers know when to give assessments and how often.				
d. Our teachers know how to analyze the results of assessment at the individual student level.				

Indicator	Beginning (B)	Emerging (E)	Systematic (S)	Sustainable (SS)
e. Our teachers know how to interpret the results of formal and informal assessments.				
f. Our teachers know how to plan instruction based on diagnosis.				
g. Our teachers know how to integrate ongoing assessment into instruction.				

3. Data Analysis—The progress we have made identifying, examining, aggregating, and disaggregating data to derive meaning for planning and targeting literacy instruction. Data include individual and group demographics and outcome and process data related to reading.

Indicator	Beginning (B)	Emerging (E)	Systematic (S)	Sustainable (SS)
a. Our teachers have knowledge of where a child should be (what good reading is).				
b. Our teachers conduct ongoing examination of reading program data using a rubric or protocol. Data include student work, supplemented as needed with tests/assessments for specific skills.				

Indicator	Beginning (B)	Emerging (E)	Systematic (S)	Sustainable (SS)
c. Our teachers interpret patterns and connections to identify opportunities for targeted interventions.				
d. Our teachers effectively implement strategies derived from scientifically based reading research; these strategies are targeted based on the analysis of student data generated from locally adopted reading curriculum.				

4. Intervention Strategies—Our progress toward providing differentiated reading instruction using scientifically based reading research and analysis of student need.

Indicator	Beginning (B)	Emerging (E)	Systematic (S)	Sustainable (SS)
a. Our teachers know the components of good first teaching of reading and can articulate principles of good reading instruction based on scientifically based research and best practice.				

4. Intervention Strategies (continued)

Indicator	Beginning (B)	Emerging (E)	Systematic (S)	Sustainable (SS)
b. Our teachers have an understanding of the adopted reading curriculum (philosophy, materials, resources, and assessments).				
c. Our teachers implement a variety of strategies that are intentional, explicit, and based on student need.				

Indicator	Beginning (B)	Emerging (E)	Systematic (S)	Sustainable (SS)
d. Our teachers use assessments and information to guide instructional decisions and practices.				

5. Support Networks—Our progress toward an organizational system that enhances the collaboration of key stakeholders.

Indicator	Beginning (B)	Emerging (E)	Systematic (S)	Sustainable (SS)
a. Our teachers and coach participate in regularly scheduled meetings to discuss scientifically based reading research practices, continue training, and share best practices.				

5. Support Networks (continued)

Indicator	Beginning (B)	Emerging (E)	Systematic (S)	Sustainable (SS)
b. Our teachers and coach engage in professional development opportunities.				
c. Our teachers and coach use technology to share information about reading issues.				
d. Our teachers and coach partner with key stakeholders.				

**Additional Comments on the
Literacy Program and Its Components:**

SAMPLE PROGRAM EVALUATION (EXTRACT)

1. Coaching—The literacy coach provides assistance to teachers at individual and group levels to ensure implementation of literacy professional learning components to promote effective instruction.

Indicator	Beginning (B)	Emerging (E)	Systematic (S)	Sustainable (SS)
a. Our literacy coach facilitates, coaches, mentors, and presents information that meets the needs and skill level of the individual or groups of teachers.	Our literacy coach has started to meet with a group of five teachers to review data on comprehension. First meeting— March 20, 2007			
b. Our literacy coach conducts focused dialogue at the individual, grade, school, or district level to promote knowledge and build skills in assessment, diagnosis, data analysis, interventions, etc.			The literacy coach meets regularly with grade K teachers to discuss phonemic awareness. She's shared several assessment procedures, and the teachers are trying them in the classroom.	

References

Adams, M. J., Foorman, B., Lundberg, I., & Beeler, T. (1998). *Phonemic awareness in young children.* Baltimore: Paul H. Brookes.

Albritton, G. (2003). *K–2 reading coaches initiative: Follow-up study at third grade.* [Online article] Retrieved September 26, 2006, from http://apps.sdhc.k12.fl.us/itsweb/asmact/evaluation/01_Follow_Up_Report.pdf

Allington, R. L. (2005). What counts as evidence in evidence-based education? *Reading Today, 23*(3), 16.

Allington, R. L. (2006, February/March). Reading specialists, reading teachers, reading coaches: A question of credentials. *Reading Today, 23*(4), 16–17.

ASCD Supervision Series. (1988). *Another set of eyes.* Alexandria, VA: Association for Supervision and Curriculum Development.

Barkley, S. (2005). *Quality teaching in a culture of coaching.* Lanham, MD: Scarecrow Education.

Bauwens, J., Hourcade, J. J., & Friend, M. (1989). Cooperative teaching: A model for general and special education integration. *Remedial and Special Education, 10*(2), 17–22.

Bean, R. (2004). *The reading specialist: Leadership for the classroom, school, and community.* New York: Guilford Press.

Bear, D. R., Invernizzi, M., Templeton, S., & Johnston, F. (2000). *Words their way: Word study for phonics, vocabulary, and spelling instruction* (3rd ed.). Upper Saddle River, NJ: Merrill.

Beck, I. L., McKeown, M. G., & Kucan, L. (2002). *Bringing words to life: Robust vocabulary instruction.* New York: Guilford Press.

Beers, K. (2002). *When kids can't read: What teachers can do.* Portsmouth, NH: Heinemann.

Birchak, B., Connor, C., Crawford, K., Kahn, L., Kaser, S., Turner, S., & Short, K. (1998). *Teacher study groups: Building community through dialogue and reflection.* Urbana, IL: National Council of Teachers of English.

Blase, J., & Blase, J. (1998). *Instructional leadership: How really good principals promote teaching and learning.* Thousand Oaks, CA: Corwin Press.

Blevins, W. (1997). *Phonemic awareness activities for early reading success.* New York: Scholastic Professional Books.

Block, C. C., & Pressley, M. (Eds.). (2002). *Comprehension instruction: Research-based best practices.* New York: Guilford Press.

Boomer, G. (1992). Negotiating the curriculum reformulated. In G. Boomer, N. Lester, C. Onore, & J. Cook (Eds.), *Negotiating the curriculum: Educating for the 21st century* (pp. 32–45). London: Falmer Press.

Borko, H., & Putnam, R. T. (1996). Learning to teach. In D. Berliner & R. Caifee (Eds.), *Handbook of research in educational psychology* (pp. 673–708). New York: McMillan.

Brunelle, M. (2005). *The impact of focused study groups on teacher collaboration and literacy instructional practices.* Available: http://escholarship.bc.edu/dissertations/AAI3173655/

Calhoun, E. (2004). *Using data to assess your reading program.* Alexandria, VA: Association for Supervision and Curriculum Development.

Carnegie Corporation of New York. (2006). *A theory of action for high school reform: A conversation with Alan Bersin.* New York: Author. Available: http://www.publicengagement.com/practices/publications/documents/bersin.pdf

Central Regional Reading First Technical Assistance Center. (2005). *An introductory guide for Reading First coaches.* Austin, TX: Vaughn Gross Center for Reading and Language Arts at the University of Texas at Austin.

Chokski, S., & Fernandez, C. (2004). Challenges to importing Japanese Lesson Study: Concerns, misconceptions and nuances. *Phi Delta Kappan, 85*(6), 520–525.

Cohen, D. K., & Hill, H. C. (2000). Instructional policy and classroom performance: The mathematics reform in California. *Teachers College Record, 102*(2), 294–343.

Cohen, D., Raudenbush, S., & Ball, D. L. (2000). *Resources, instruction, and research.* Washington, DC: Center for the Study of Teaching and Policy.

Cook, L., & Friend, M. (1995). Co-teaching: Guidelines for creating effective practices. *Focus on Exceptional Children, 28*(3), 1–16.

Cordingley, P., & Bell, M. (2002). Summary of the Consortia Overview Report 2002. National College for School Leadership. [Online article] Retrieved September 22, 2006, from https://www.ncsl.org.uk/index.cfm

Costa, A. L., & Garmston, R. J. (Program Consultants). (1988). *Another set of eyes: Techniques for classroom observation* [Videotape]. Alexandria, VA: Association for Supervision and Curriculum Development.

Costa, A. L., & Garmston, R. J. (2002). *Cognitive coaching: A foundation for renaissance schools.* Norwood, MA: Christopher-Gordon Publishers.

Cunningham, P. M. (1999). *Phonics they use: Words for reading and writing.* Boston: Allyn & Bacon.

Cushman, K. (1996, November). Looking collaboratively at student work: An essential toolkit. *Horace, 13*(2). Available: http://www.essentialschools.org/cs/resources/view/ces_res/57

Cushman, K. (1998, March). How friends can be critical as schools make essential change. *Horace, 14*(5). Available: http://www.essentialschools.org/cs/resources/view/ces_res/43

Danielson, C. (1996). *Enhancing professional practice: A framework for teaching.* Alexandria, VA: Association for Supervision and Curriculum Development.

Darling-Hammond, L. (1998, February). Teacher learning that supports student learning. *Educational Leadership, 55*(5), 6–11.

Darling-Hammond, L. (2003, May). Keeping good teachers: Why it matters, what leaders can do. *Educational Leadership, 60*(8), 6–13.

Darling-Hammond, L., & McLaughlin, M. W. (1995, April). Policies that support professional development in an era of reform. *Phi Delta Kappan, 96*(8), 597–604.

Davis, C., & Wilcock, E. (2006). *Teaching materials using case studies* [Online article]. 12 Guides for Lecturers Series. Liverpool, England: Higher Education Academy, UK Centre for Materials Education, University of Liverpool. Available: http://www.materials.ac.uk/guides/casestudies.asp

DeFord, D., Morgan, D. N., Saylor-Crowder, K., Pae, T., Johnson, R., Stephens, D., Donnelly, A., & Hamel, E. (2003). *Changes in children's cue and strategy use during reading: Findings from the first year of professional development in the South Carolina Reading Initiative* (Technical Report #002). Retrieved September 26, 2006, from http://www.ncte.org/profdev/onsite/readinit/groups/110385.htm?source=gs

Desimone, L., Porter, A., Garet, M., Yoon, K., & Birman, B. (2002). Effects of professional development on teachers' instruction: Results from a three-year longitudinal study. *Educational Evaluation and Policy Analysis, 24*(2), 81–112.

Deussen, T., Coskie, T., Robinson, L., & Autio, E. (2007). *"Coach" can mean many things: Five categories of literacy coaches in Reading First.* Washington, DC: U.S. Department of Education Institute of Educational Sciences National Center for Education Evaluation and Regional Assistance. Available: http://ies.ed.gov/ncee/edlabs/regions/northwest/pdf/REL_2007005.pdf

Duncan, M. (2006). *Literacy coaching: Developing effective teachers through instructional dialogue.* Katonah, NY: R. C. Owen Publishers.

Education Commission of the States. (2000). *Informing practices and improving results with data-driven decisions.* Available: http://www.ecs.org/clearinghouse/24/02/2402.htm

Elmore, R. F. (1997). *Investing in teacher learning: Staff development and instructional improvement in Community School District #2.* New York: National Commission on Teaching and America's Future.

Elmore, R. F., & Burney, D. (1997). *School variation and systemic instructional improvement in Community School District #2.* New York: Learning Research and Development Center, High Performance Learning Communities Project.

Farr, R., & Greene, B. (1999). *A guide for evaluating a reading or language arts program.* Bloomington, IN: Center for Innovation in Assessment. Available: http://www.doe.state.in.us/publications/pdf-early/EVALREAD.pdf

Feagin, J., Orum, A., & Sjoberg, G. (Eds.). (1991). *A case for case study.* Chapel Hill: University of North Carolina Press.

Fernandez, C., Cannon, J., & Chokski, S. (2003). A U.S.–Japanese lesson study collaboration reveals critical lenses for examining practice. *Teaching and Teacher Education, 19,* 171–185.

Fielding, A., Schoenbach, R., & Jordan, M. (Eds.). (2003). *Building academic literacy: Lessons from reading apprenticeship classrooms grades 6–12.* San Francisco: Jossey-Bass.

Fox, D. (2004, June). Guiding instruction through assessment. *Leadership: Magazine of the Association of California School Administrators.* Available: http://www.acsa.org/publications/pub_detail.cfm?leadershipPubID=1427

Friend, M., & Cook, L. (1996). *Interactions: Collaboration skills for school professionals* (2nd ed.). White Plains, NY: Longman.

Fullan, M. (2001). *Leading in a culture of change.* San Francisco: Jossey-Bass.

General Teaching Council for England. (n.d.). *Continuing professional development—Learning conversations.* Retrieved on September 26, 2006, from http://www.gtce.org.uk/cpd_home/learningconversation/dulwich

Gersten, R., Morvant, M., & Brengelman, S. (1995). Close to the classroom is close to the bone: Coaching as a means to translate research into classroom practice. *Exceptional Children, 62*(1), 52–56.

Gersten, R., Vaughn, S., Deschler, D., & Schiller, E. (1997). What we know about using research findings: Implications for improving special education practice. *Journal of Learning Disabilities, 30,* 466–476.

Gottesman, B. (2000). *Peer coaching for educators.* Lanham, MD: Scarecrow Education.

Graves, M. (2005). *The vocabulary book: Learning and instruction.* New York: Teachers College Press.

Guskey, T. R. (1990, February). Integrating innovations. *Educational Leadership, 47*(5), 11–15.

Guskey, T. R. (2000). *Evaluating professional development.* Thousand Oaks, CA: Corwin.

Guskey, T. R. (2002, November). Does it make a difference? Evaluating professional development. *Educational Leadership, 59*(3), 45–51.

Guthrie, J., Wigfield, A., & Perencevich, K. (2004). *Motivating reading comprehension: Concept-oriented reading instruction.* Mahwah, NJ: Lawrence Erlbaum Associates.

Hammerness, K., Shulman, L., & Darling-Hammond, L. (2000). Learning from cases [Online article]. Available: http://gallery.carnegiefoundation.org/collections/castl_he/khammerness/bground/bground.html

Harvard Family Research Project. (2005/2006, Winter). Questions and answers: A conversation with Thomas Guskey. *The Evaluation Exchange, XI*(4). Available: http://www.gse.harvard.edu/hfrp/eval/issue32/qanda.htm

Harvey, S., & Goudvis, A. (2000). *Strategies that work: Teaching comprehension to enhance understanding.* York, ME: Stenhouse.

Hays, L. J., & Harris, C. D. (n.d.). Using literacy coaching as a means to change science teachers' attitudes about teaching writing: A case study [Online article]. Available:http://www2.sjsu.edu/elementaryed/ejlts/archives/school_practice/Lesliehays.html

Hiebert, J., Gallimore, R., & Stigler, J. W. (2002). A knowledge base for the teaching profession: What would it look like and how can we get one? *Educational Researcher, 31*(5), 3–15.

Hiskes, D. G. (2007). *Reading pathways: Simple exercises to improve reading fluency.* San Francisco: Jossey-Bass.

International Reading Association. (2004). *The role and qualifications of the reading coach in the United States: A position statement of the International Reading Association.* Newark, DE: IRA.

International Reading Association. (2006a). IRA surveys coaches. *Reading Today, 23*(5), 1–3. Available: http://www.reading.org/publications/reading_today/samples/RTY-0604-surveys.html

International Reading Association. (2006b). *Standards for middle and high school literacy coaches.* Newark, DE: Author. Available: http://www.reading.org/resources/issues/reports/coaching.html

International Reading Association. (2007). *IRA style guide: Standards for reading professionals.* Available: http://www.reading.org/styleguide/standards_reading_profs.html

Joyce, B., & Showers, B. (2002). *Student achievement through staff development* (3rd ed.). Alexandria, VA: Association for Supervision and Curriculum Development.

Kannapel, P. J., & Clements, S. K. (2005). *Inside the black box of high-performing, high-poverty schools.* Lexington, KY: Prichard Committee for Academic Excellence.

Keene, E. O., & Zimmermann, S. (1997). *Mosaic of thought: Teaching comprehension in a reader's workshop.* Portsmouth, NH: Heinemann.

Killion, J. (2002). *Assessing impact: Evaluating staff development.* Oxford, OH: National Staff Development Council.

Killion, J. (2003, Fall). 8 smooth steps: Solid footwork makes evaluation of staff development programs a song. *Journal of Staff Development, 24*(4), 14–21.

Killion, J. (2005/2006, Winter). Evaluating the impact of professional development in eight steps. *The Evaluation Exchange, XI*(4). Available: http://www.gse.harvard.edu/hfrp/eval/issue32/spotlight1.html

Killion, J., & Harrison, C. (2005, October). Role: Data coach. *T3: Teachers Teaching Teachers, 1*(2). Available: http://nsdc.org or by calling 800-727-7288.

Knight, M. J. (2007). *Instructional coaching: A partnership approach to improving instruction.* Thousand Oaks, CA: Corwin Press.

Lachat, M. A., & Smith, S. (2005). Practices that support data use in urban high schools. *Journal of Education for Students Placed at Risk, 10*(3), 333–349.

Larner, M. (2004). *Pathways: Charting a course for professional learning.* Portsmouth, NH: Heinemann.

Learning First Alliance. (2000). *Every child reading: A professional development guide.* Washington, DC: Author. Available: http://www.learningfirst.org/publications/reading/

Levesque, J., & Carnahan, D. (2005). *Stepping stones to evaluating your own school literacy program.* Naperville, IL: Learning Point Associates.

Lewis, C. (2002, November/December). What are the essential elements of lesson study? *The CSP connection, 2*(6), 1, 4. Available: http://csmp.ucop.edu/downloads/csp/newsletters/newsletter11_2002.pdf

Lewis, C., Perry, R., & Hurd, J. (2004, February). A deeper look at lesson study. *Educational Leadership, 61*(5), 6–11.

Little, J. W. (1982). Norms of collegiality and experimentation: Workplace conditions of school success. *American Educational Research Journal, 19*(3), 325–340.

Little, J. W. (1993). Teachers' professional development in a climate of educational reform. *Educational Evaluation and Policy Analysis, 15,* 129–151.

Lock, K. (2006). Dear colleague, please come for a visit. *T3: Teachers Teaching Teachers, 2*(2).

Looking at Student Work [Web site]. http://www.lasw.org

Lord, B. (1994). Teachers' professional development: Critical colleagueship and the role of professional communities. In N. Cobb (Ed.), *The future of education: Perspectives on national standards in America* (pp. 175–204). New York: College Entrance Examination Board.

Lyons, C., & Pinnell, G. (2001). *Systems for change in literacy education: A guide to professional development.* Portsmouth, NH: Heinemann.

Maryland Department of Education (n.d.). *Analyzing and using data* [Online toolkit]. Available: http://www.mdk12.org/data/index.html

Maryland Department of Education. (n.d.) *Lead data dialogues: Examining your monitoring data.* [Online article]. Available: http://www.mdk12.org/data/course/m4w3/pr3/

Marzano, R. (2003). *What works in schools: Translating research into action.* Alexandria, VA: Association for Supervision and Curriculum Development.

Marzano, R. J. (2007). *The art and science of teaching: A comprehensive framework for effective instruction.* Alexandria, VA: Association for Supervision and Curriculum Development.

McKenna, M. C., & Stahl, S. A. (2003). *Assessment for reading instruction.* New York: Guilford Press.

Meyer, R. J. (1996). *Teachers' study group: Forum for collective thought, meaning-making, and action.* Paper presented at the Annual Meeting of the American Educational Research Association, New York, NY, April 8–13, 1996. (ERIC Document Reproduction Service No. 394 952)

Meyer, R. J. (1998). *Composing a teacher study group: Learning about inquiry in primary classrooms.* Mahwah, NJ: Lawrence Erlbaum Associates.

Mid-continent Research for Education and Learning. (n.d.) *Leadership folio series: Sustaining school improvement.* Denver, CO: Author. Available: http://www.mcrel.org/PDF/LeadershipOrganizationDevelopment/5031TG_datafolio.pdf

Moats, L. C. (1999, June). *Teaching reading IS rocket science: What expert teachers of reading should know and be able to do.* Washington, DC: American Federation of Teachers. Available: http://www.aft.org/pubs-reports/downloads/teachers/rocketsci.pdf

Morocco, C. C., & Aguilar, C. M. (2002). Coteaching for content understanding: A schoolwide model. *Journal of Educational and Psychological Consultation, 13*(4), 315–347.

Moscovitch, E. (2006). *2005 Evaluation of the Alabama Reading Initiative.* Montgomery, AL: Alabama Department of Education. Available: http://www.alsde.edu/html/sections/doc_download.asp?section=50&id=5716&sort=40

Murata, R. (2002). What does team teaching mean? A case study of interdisciplinary learning. *Journal of Educational Research, 96*(2), 67–77.

National College for School Leadership. (n.d.). *Mentoring and coaching for learning: Questions for schools.* London: Author. Available: http://www.ncsl.org.uk/media/2FC/0F/randd-coaching-dfes-questions.pdf

National School Reform Faculty. (2006). *Critical friends groups: Frequently asked questions.* London: Author. Available: http://www.nsrfharmony.org/faq.html

Neufeld, B., & Roper, D. (2003). *Coaching: A strategy for developing instructional capacity.* Providence, RI: Aspen Institute Program on Education and the Annenberg Institute for School Reform.

No Child Left Behind (NCLB) Act of 2001 (Public Law 107–110). Text available: http://www.ed.gov/policy/elsec/leg/esea02/index.html

Northwest Regional Educational Laboratory. (2005, Fall). Having "'another set of eyeballs": Critical friends groups. *Teachers Working Together, 11*(1). Available: http://www.nwrel.org/nwedu/11-01/cfg/

Ohio Department of Education. (2006). *Literacy specialist endorsement submission guidelines.* Available: http://www.ode.state.oh.us

Partners in School Innovation. (n.d.). *Theory of action.* [Online article]. Available: http://www.partnersin-schools.org/program/theory.html

Porter, A.C., Garet, M. S., Desimone, L., Yoon, K. S., & Birman, B. (2000). *Does professional development change teacher practice? Results from a three-year study.* Washington, DC: American Institute for Research in the Behavioral Sciences. (ERIC Document Reproduction Service No. ED455227)

Pressley, M., Allington, R. L., Wharton-McDonald, R., Block, C. C., & Morrow, L. M. (2001). *Learning to read: Lessons from exemplary first-grade classrooms.* New York: Guilford Press.

Rasinski, T. (2003). *The fluent reader: Oral reading strategies for building word recognition, fluency, and comprehension*. New York: Scholastic Professional Books.

Rasinski, T., Blachowicz, C., & Lems, K. (Eds.). (2006). *Fluency instruction: Research-based best practices*. New York: Guilford Press.

Ray, K. W. (1999). *Wondrous words: Writers and writing in the elementary school*. Urbana, IL: National Council of Teachers of English.

Reinhiller, N. (1996). Co-teaching: New variations on a not-so-new practice. *Teacher Education and Special Education, 19*, 34–48.

Research for Better Schools (RBS) [Web site]. http://www.rbs.org

Richardson, J. (2001, December/January). Lesson study: Japanese method benefits all teachers. *Results*. Available: http://www.nsdc.org/library/publications/results/res12-00rich.cfm

Rivkin, S. G., Hanushek, E. A., & Kain, J. F. (2005). Teachers, schools, and academic achievement. *The Econometric Society, 73*(2), 417–458.

Robbins, P. (1991). *How to implement a peer coaching program*. Alexandria, VA: Association for Supervision and Curriculum Development.

Samway, K. D. (2006). *When English language learners write: Connecting research to practice K–8*. Portsmouth, NH: Heinemann.

Sanders, W. L., & Rivers, J. C. (1996). *Cumulative and residual effects of teachers on future student academic achievement*. Knoxville: University of Tennessee.

Sather, S. (2004). *The Spokane school district: Intentionally building capacity that leads to increased student achievement: Theory of action*. Available: http://www.nwrel.org/scpd/re-engineering/SpokaneSD/TheoryAction.asp

Schmoker, M. (1999). *Results: The key to continuous school improvement* (2nd ed.). Alexandria, VA: Association for Supervision and Curriculum Development.

Schmoker, M. (2003, February). First things first: Demystifying data analysis. *Educational Leadership, 60*(5), 22–24.

Schmoker, M. (2004). Tipping point: From feckless reform to substantive instructional improvement. *Phi Delta Kappan, 85*(6), 424–432.

Schoenbach, R., Greenleaf, C., Cziko, C., & Hurwitz, L. (1999). *Reading for understanding: A guide to improving reading in middle and high school classrooms*. Indianapolis, IN: Jossey-Bass Teacher.

School District of Philadelphia. (n.d.). *Sample data analysis protocol*. Available: http://phila.schoolnet.com/outreach/philadelphia/teachersstaff/protocols/

Sevakis, P., & Harris, G. (1992). Co-teaching: Using the expertise of regular and special education for language arts instruction and remediation. *Reading and Writing Quarterly: Overcoming Learning Disabilities, 8*, 57–70.

Shulman, J. (1991). Revealing the mysteries of teacher-written cases: Opening the black box. *Journal of Teacher Education, 42*(4), 250–262.

Shulman, J. (2002). *Happy accidents: Cases as opportunities for teacher learning*. Available: http://www.wested.org/online_pubs/happyaccidents.pdf

Shulman, L. (1987). Knowledge and teaching: Foundations of the new reform. *Harvard Educational Review, 57*(1), 1–22.

Slater, C. L., & Simmons, D. L. (2001). The design and implementation of a peer coaching program. *American Secondary Education, 29*(3), 67–76.

Small Schools Project. (n.d.). *Tools*. Available: http://smallschoolsproject.org/index.asp?siteloc=tool&section=guidelines

Snow, C., Griffin, P., & Burns, M. S. (2005). *Knowledge to support the teaching of reading: Preparing teachers for a changing world*. San Francisco: Jossey-Bass.

Stahl, S., & Kapinus, B. (2001). *Word power: What every educator needs to know about teaching vocabulary*. Washington, DC: National Education Association.

Teachers College, Columbia University–Lesson Study Research Group [Web site]. http://www.tc.edu/lessonstudy/worksamples.html

Tobin, K., & Wolff-Roth, M. (2005). Implementing coteaching and cogenerative dialoguing in urban science education. *School Science and Mathematics, 105*(6), 313–321.

Torgesen, J., Meadows, J. G., & Howard, P. (n.d.). *Using student outcome data to help guide professional development and teacher support: Issues for Reading First and K–12 reading plans.* A report from the Florida Center for Reading Research. Available: http://www.fcrr.org/assessment/pdf/Prof_dev_guided.pdf

U.S. Department of Education, Office of Elementary and Secondary Education. (2002, April). *Guidance for the Reading First program.* Washington, DC: Author. Available: http://www.ed.gov/programs/readingfirst/guidance.pdf

Vaughn, S., Elbaum, B. E., Schumm, J. S., & Hughes, M. T. (1998). Social outcomes for students with and without learning disabilities in inclusive classrooms. *Journal of Learning Disabilities, 31,* 428–436.

Vygotsky, L. S. (1978). *Mind and society: The development of higher mental processes.* Cambridge, MA: Harvard University Press.

Walpole, S. (2004). *Literacy coaches: Practice in search of research.* Available: http://www.ciera.org/library/presos/2004/csi/swal.pdf

Walpole, S., & McKenna, M. C. (2004). *The literacy coach's handbook: A guide to research-based practice.* New York: Guilford Press.

Weaver, M. K., Rentsch, J., & Calliari, M. (2004). The Saginaw teacher study group movement: From pilot to districtwide study groups in four years. *The National Writing Project at Work Models of Inservice Series, 1*(6). Berkeley: National Writing Project, University of California. Available: http://www.writingproject.org/cs/nwpp/print/nwpr/2182

Weisburd, C., & Sniad, T. (2005/2006, Winter). Evaluations to watch: Theory of action in practice. *The Evaluation Exchange, XI*(4). Available: http://www.gse.harvard.edu/hfrp/eval/issue32/eval3.html

Wellman, B., & Lipton, L. (2004). *Facilitating data driven dialogue: A facilitator's guide to collaborative inquiry.* Sherman, CT: MiraVia, LLC.

Westat. (2005). *The secretary's fourth annual report on teacher quality: A highly qualified teacher in every classroom.* Retrieved September 27, 2006, from http://www.ed.gov/about/reports/annual/teachprep/2005Title2-Report.pdf

Wilhelm, J. D. (2004). *Reading is seeing.* New York: Scholastic Publishers.

Wolff-Roth, M., & Tobin, K. (Eds.). (2005). *Teaching together, learning together.* New York: Peter Lang.

Wright, S. P., Horn, S. P., & Sanders, W. L. (1997). Teacher and classroom context effects on students' achievement: Implications for evaluation. *Journal of Personnel Evaluation in Education, 11,* 57–67.

Index

Note: An *f* after a page number indicates a reference to a figure.

About the Author

Mary Catherine Moran has nearly 30 years of experience in the field of education as a classroom teacher, a professional development provider for teachers who work with students with disabilities, and a literacy coach. She has an M.S. in reading from the State University College at Albany, an M.S. in special education from Syracuse University. She is permanently certified in New York State in reading, special education, and elementary education. In her current position as Senior Literacy Specialist at the State University of New York College at Oneonta, she has been instrumental in assisting state and local education agencies with high-leverage training and support of literacy coaches in North Carolina, Ohio, Pennsylvania, and New Jersey. Mary Catherine's work with literacy coaches focuses on using student data to inform instruction and providing a continuum of professional learning opportunities. She has also managed state and local projects related to curriculum alignment, differentiated instruction, and school reform.

You may contact the author via e-mail at marycatherine.moran@gmail.com or via regular mail at Eastern Stream Center, State University College at Oneonta, Bugbee Hall, Oneonta, New York 13820. For additional resources on literacy coaching, consult the Eastern Stream Web site at www.easternstream.org.

Related ASCD Resources: Literacy

At the time of publication, the following ASCD resources were available (ASCD stock numbers appear in parentheses). For the most up-to-date information about ASCD resources, go to www.ascd.org.

Audios

Improving Literacy CD Bundle with Diane Wheeler; Carla Lovett, Lisa Churchwell, and Lendy Willis; James Stack and Lydia Stack; Linda Cornwell; and Judith Irvin, Melinda Dukes, and Julie Meltzer (#506147)

Promoting Literacy Achievement Audio CD Bundle with Garry Buekcert; Joan Baldwin and Sue Pedro; John Savage and Cindy Strickland; Lucinda Riedle; and Richard Allington, Jennifer Graff, Luneta Williams, and Courtney Zmach (#505384)

Books

Literacy Leadership for Grades 5–12 by Rosemarye Taylor and Valerie Doyle Collins (#103022)

Research-Based Methods of Reading Instruction, Grades K–3 by Sharon Vaughn and Sylvia Linan-Thompson (#104134)

Taking Action on Adolescent Literacy: An Implementation Guide for School Leaders by Judith Irvin, Julie Meltzer, and Melinda Dukes (#107034)

The Threads of Reading: Strategies for Literacy Development by Karen Tankersley (#103316)

Magazines and Newsletters

Educational Leadership: Redefining Literacy (entire issue, October 1999, #199291)

Educational Leadership: What Research Says About Reading (entire issue, March 2004, #104028)

"Spreading the Word: Literacy Coaches Share Comprehension Strategies" (*Education Update,* February 2005, Volume 47, Number 2, #105109)

Online

Visit the ASCD Web site (www.ascd.org) for the following professional development opportunities:

Creating an Effective Secondary Reading Program by Tracy Wilson (#PD06OC57)

Successful Strategies for Literacy and Learning by Angelika Machi (#PD03OC27)

Videos and Mixed Media

The Lesson Collection: Literacy Strategies, Tapes 49–56 (eight 10- to 20-minute videotapes) (#405160)

Literacy Across the Curriculum (professional development planner and resource package) (#703400)

For more information: send e-mail to member@ascd.org; call 1-800-933-2723 or 703-578-9600, press 2; send a fax to 703-575-5400; or write to Information Services, ASCD, 1703 N. Beauregard St., Alexandria, VA 22311-1714 USA.